THE
DNA
OF
BUSINESS
RELATIONSHIPS

How to Engage Expand and Energize Relationships

LINDSAY ADAMS

The
DNA
of
Business Relationships

How to Engage
Expand and Energize
Relationships

Lindsay Adams

Disclaimer: Every effort has been made to ensure this book is as accurate and complete as possible, however there may be errors both typographical and in content. The author and the publisher shall not be held liable or responsible to any person or entity with respect to any loss or damage caused or alleged to have been caused directly or indirectly by the information contained in this book.

Books may be purchased in quantity and/or special sales by contacting Lindsay Adams by email at lindsay@lindsayadams.com or by visiting our website at www.lindsayadams.com

ISBN: 978-0-6482069-1-0 - e-Book (Australia)
ISBN: 978-0-6482069-0-3 – Paperback (Australia)
ISBN: 978-198-12-8777-2 - Paperback (United States)

Library of Congress Number: 2017918761

A catalouge record for this book is available from the National Library of Australia

Published by Teamocracy
Book Cover Design by Armend Meha
Images by Shutterstock

For more information about our other products, keynote speeches and seminars please contact Lindsay at lindsay@lindsayadams.com

Table of Contents

Chapter 1

Why the DNA of Business Relationships?

Mobile devices are ruining our ability to communicate effectively on a one to one basis. We're quickly heading for a world where people are becoming more and more impersonal, the very technology that was designed to help us, has created the beginnings of the destruction of human interaction.

Do you own a mobile phone? What about a tablet computer, or perhaps a Kindle book reading device? Have you noticed how these devices have inserted themselves so easily into our lives, that they often come between simple communication now.

Think about this for a moment, as you read this book are you in love? I'm serious, do you have a husband, wife or perhaps just a significant other that you love with all your heart? I sure do, I'm married and I have had two beautiful children with my wife. I love them all to bits, though there are times when you might be confused what I love more, them or my mobile phone!

I want to challenge you here dear reader, do you love your significant other more or perhaps at times are you more in love with your mobile phone? Be honest now. In fact, let me ask, where is your mobile phone right now and where is your significant other? I bet your phone is closer than they are to your body right at this minute. Our phones are hardly ever much further away than an arm's reach.

I spoke at a conference in South Africa recently and learned that most of the speakers had left their husbands or wives at home yet none of them have left home without their mobile device. Well, it's the modern world Lindsay, I hear you say, of course we take our phones, we have to keep in touch.

True, though I did notice that while my colleagues were speaking, many of the audiencewere quietly caressing their phones, checking the screen for messages, maybe a quick look at Facebook, perhaps answering an urgent email.

Mobile phones, tablets and computers in general have downgraded the quality of our communication. We don't have proper conversations anymore, we send emails, text messages or we What's App each other, we just don't talk face to face any more.

Remember those two kids I mentioned earlier, well they are both married and even better still, they left home when they got married! Woohoo! I'm even more delighted to tell you my daughter has a little boy, Finlay, at the time of writing, he's 19 months and my son has a little girl, Elsie and she's just 9 months. Bliss, being a Grandparent is such fun.

In our family, we have this lovely tradition, called Friday Night Family Night. The kids come home for dinner, a free meal at Mum & Dad's. We get to hear all about what they got up to in the previous week and we also get to hang with our grandkids.

The week before I flew to South Africa, the kids came over and we're all sitting around the kitchen table having a drink and some snacks before dinner, my wife is preparing the meal. She comes over from the stove and says, I better get my phone. I look up and it's then it hit me. My daughter, her husband, my son, his wife and worst of all me are all sitting at the table with our mobile phones in our hand, doing Facebook, playing games or whatever!

None of us were really talking to each other, we were all together, yet we weren't really talking to each other, we were just screen surfing.

Our ability to communicate freely, that is human to human has been severely impaired by screens. It's not good enough, it has to change, we have to reconcile our relationships with these devices and figure out who is more important, our fellow human beings or our devices.

Technology is a double-edged sword, the speed at which we can communicate is now amazing. We send an email and moments later it appears in someone's inbox on the other side of the world. This is both good and bad.

Has this ever happened to you, you get a phone call from a colleague to say I just sent you an email, have you seen it? Our communication is becoming so instantaneous that we expect almost instant responses. Yet we now no longer talk face to face with each other.

This is the reason I wrote this book, to arrest the decline in the true art of conversation and relationship building in business. Let's focus in on relationships in business then.

Have you ever been to a business function and met someone for the first time and struggled to have a conversation with them? Perhaps you are the kind of person that just dreads going to business events, because you always get stuck beside the bore who just talks and talks about nothing in particular and you can never seem to get away from them. Maybe you are like 25% of the population that call themselves introverts and aren't good at mixing with strangers and find attending a business function a torturous event.

In my experience people attend functions because they know they must, yet they don't seem to know how to open up a conversation and quickly get into a relationship with other attendees. It's amazing to see the number of people hovering at the sides of the room, pretending to do something important on their phone. Like all skills some people find this easy, while others struggle. Building relationship skills is something that can be learned and the more you practice, the better you get at meeting strangers, starting a conversation and quickly moving into an engaging business relationship.

I've worked on the people side of business now for 25 years as a human resources professional and then as a self-employed conference speaker and workshop facilitator. For many years, I ran team building programs with teams which were broken and needed fixing or adjusting to some degree. I've also delivered leadership and management training and coached leaders to become better at their craft. In more recent years I've been drawn more and more toward sales and the sales process.

There is a common element to all of these activities and the common element is relationships. If you want to be a good leader or better still a great leader, you need to be in a great relationship with your people. Interestingly, some people do this better than others, almost innately and yet others need to be taught the skills of leadership. As a result of my experiences in working with people I began to wonder why is this relationship ability built in to some people and not in others?

If you want to work in a team which functions well and achieve its goals or outcomes, you have to be in a healthy relationship with your co-workers. If you are a sales person and want to make sales, or get on board quickly with your prospects and turn them into clients; you must be in a good relationship. Relationships underpin all of these activities and the more I investigated, the more it became clear that relationships are the foundation for most people-oriented business activities. What made me even more curious though was whether or not some people had a relationship gene; that is, a built-in talent to engage with others. Was it built into their DNA?

I began to read and investigate and created models that accurately reflected relationships as I saw them. The key I found was in the first stages of the relationship. If you could quickly engage with people, then you had a greater chance of getting what you needed or wanted from the relationship.

Could these talents, habits or behaviours be so deep down in some people's natural connectors, that it was part of their DNA? Passed to them by their ancestors and a building block of their personality and behavioural model? Or was it a learned behaviour influenced by their upbringing or environment? Out of sheer curiosity I began to research and investigate human DNA.

Deoxyribonucleic acid is the hereditary material in all humans and almost all other organisms. It carries the genetic instructions used in the growth, development and functioning of most living organisms and even viruses. It is a two-stranded molecule and has a unique double helix shape, a lot like a twisted ladder. There are four basic building blocks contained in DNA called adenine, cytosine, guanine and thymine. The bases of one strand of the DNA molecule pair together with complimentary bases on the opposite strand of DNA to form the rungs of the DNA ladder. The order and sequence of these four building blocks form the instructions for the genome: our genetic make-up. They determine our physical, physiological and emotional behavioural traits.

OK, science lesson over, why am I telling you this? I think that relationship building and relationship nurturing is just plain built in to some people. I'm one of those people. Relationships are in my DNA and I have evidence that it was passed to me by my mother and shows up clearly in some of my brothers and their behaviours in the world today. More on that later.

I began to think more about my genetic make-up, my DNA and ponder how relationships had impacted my experiences at so many key turning points throughout my life. I began to cast my thoughts back over my experiences and unpack what I do when creating new relationships. Probably the most intense and effective period I ever spent building relationships quickly was when I built the house I live in.

It was 24 years ago and quite an adventure for a guy who worked by day as a human resources professional in the Australian Tax Office. The more I pondered on that project, the clearer it became that I had identified the key elements to building successful relationships. Not only that, these elements were built into my DNA. Constructing worthwhile relationships are actually built into my makeup.

These elements when combined, worked well and could be easily modelled by others to achieve similar outcomes to what I had achieved. Even more interesting is the fact that scientists from Stanford University Department of genetics believe that DNA can change as much as up to 20% due to a natural process called 'methylation'. This happens as we get older and affects the DNA of our offspring.

What that means is that even if relationships are not built into your system you can learn how to adopt the elements and perhaps your DNA may change with age and experience. Whether your DNA changes or not is really immaterial, the important piece here is that if you follow these simple yet powerful elements, you will be able to get into relationship quickly with people and then get what you need or want. It's not about manipulation, it is genuinely about entering into a mutually beneficial relationship, creating a win/win situation with full honesty and integrity.

Once I had 'unpacked' what I had done and identified these elements I was stunned by two things:

1.   The elements were so simple, anyone could do it, and

2. Even though it was so simple, many people still lived in fear of creating positive relationships that would best serve them and the other person.

It became clear to me that a lot of people live in fear of relationships. They don't know what to say and they are frozen with fear when it comes to making conversation and moving forward after the basic introductions are made. It came down to what was a person's safety zone versus meeting other people in the hope that they might win some business.

The more I thought about it, I identified three basic fears people have when it comes to making new relationships.

The Three Fears:

1. I'm afraid to talk to successful influential people.

2. I'm afraid of rejection by others.

3. I'm afraid I'll look silly, nonprofessional or worse amateurish.

I've been to hundreds if not thousands of events and observed people engaging with others for the first time or perhaps for the twenty-first time. I've worked with organisations, training and coaching their staff on what to say and do at events in order to get into relationship quickly and I've found that these fears are real for some people.

One typical example comes to mind, which sums up a lot of what happens at business events. I was working with a small engineering firm in Brisbane; the owner is a likeable guy and gets on easily with other people. He has built a successful practice largely on his name and reputation and his ability to meet people and quickly build relationships to a point where they want to do business with him. The business has now grown to fifteen staff, so isn't large by any means, though they are successful.

The owner recognised it was time perhaps to take on a partner and move to the next level, and he had two guys in the business who were prime candidates for the role. We discussed these two options and he lamented that both of them were hopeless at meeting and engaging with potential clients at industry events. Apparently, they would attend an event together, sit at a table together, talk to each other and when the event was over, leave together without making any connections with other attendees. Chances are you've seen this or even done it yourself?

The scenario he described was exactly what I had observed time and time again at business events across Brisbane, Australia and in fact the world. People are comfortable talking with people they know and they are scared witless when it comes to engaging with a stranger.

Let's examine the three fears; were these guys afraid of meeting successful, influential people? Perhaps. There were sometimes influential people at the events they attended. I think it was more they were afraid of rejection or worse making a fool of themselves and looking silly at a professional event.

OVERCOMING YOUR BLOCKS

There are ways to overcome your blocks and it takes the form of implementing some simple elements to enhance your relationships:

I actually built a house using these elements, only at the time I didn't have a relationship model in mind, I just knew that if I was going to do this project, I wanted to work with trusted friends or friends of friends. As the project unfolded, so did my expertise at building and managing relationships. It's only now, twenty something years later that I have unpacked what I did and documented these elements to share with others.

The 10 Step Relationships Guy Model

It's only in recent times that I've begun to focus more and more on relationships. People often compliment me on how good I am at building relationships and keeping in touch with people. A good friend once called me "The Relationships Guy" and that term has stuck to me ever since. I have been developing "The Relationships Guy - 10 Step Relationships Model" for some time and here it is laid out for you to see and better still, put into action for yourself.

I've broken it into steps and some steps you can jump over or work through quicker than others. I've written as if you are attending a networking or business function, however the process applies to all situations where you meet someone for the first or perhaps even the twenty-first time. I'm not going to explain the whole model in detail here, instead, I'll give you the major headings and you can then read the following chapters for the finer points.

The 10 Step Relationships Guy Model

Step 1   You Meet Someone at a Function

Typically, when we meet for the first time you would shake hands and introduce yourself. You would say your name and ask for their name. Next you may ask what they do and perhaps share what you do. These are the typical basics of a beginning conversation. The next step is where a lot of people come unstuck.

Step 2   Listen More, Talk Less

When you are talking to the person, you must focus on them 100%, listen carefully and hang on their every word. Treat this conversation as the most important conversation you've had all day.

Step 3 Swap Business Cards

If you've had a meaningful conversation you may want to swap business cards. This is almost expected in most networking situations though by no means mandatory. I suggest you only swap cards after a meaningful conversation and you want to keep in touch with the other party. A lot of people I meet today have their card out almost as soon as we've shaken hands. In Asia, it's very normal to exchange "name cards" after you introduce yourself.

Step 4 Ask Clever Questions

Once you are past the initial greetings, a real relationships master will get the other person talking as much as possible. Apply the good old 80/20 rule here, have them talking about 80% of the time, while you talk about 20%. In order to do this easily, you must become skilled at asking clever questions, these are the questions that open up a conversation and encourage the other person to talk more.

Step 5 Find the Common Ground.

A simple way to prolong the conversation is to find the common ground. That is: find out what you and the other person have in common. Do you both follow the same sporting team, do you both have the same car, the same number of children, the same holiday location? The list goes on! Talking about something you both know and are interested in, is a whole lot easier than struggling with a topic you don't know much about.

Step 6 P.S. Positive Service

An act of positive service goes a long way. Offer to refill their coffee cup, introduce them to someone else in the room who would be a good connection for them or send them an article you have read that would help them. There are lots of ways to serve, you just need to keep your eyes and ears open for an opportunity.

Step 7   Can I Do Business with This Person?

If you are at a business networking function, it's well known that everyone present is on the lookout for business opportunities. However, any function is a good opportunity to source a good business opportunity. As you are speaking to the person, you must figure out if you could do business with them. That is: either they could buy or provide a service for you, or you could buy or provide a service for them. Figure this out first. If the answer is no, go on to the next step.

The next step is to figure out if this person is someone with whom one of your Key 4 buddies could do business. A Key 4 buddy is someone that you trust and support and shares the same target market as you do, though is not in competition with you. You can easily refer business to them and vice versa. Perhaps this person could do business with a business buddy of yours? Figure this out next. If the answer is yes, keep talking and move on to Step 8 and Step 9.

If they aren't a prospect for you or one of your business buddies, stop talking to them and politely move on! Sounds mercenary, however you are there to network and find business opportunities, so go talk to someone with whom you can do business.

One final caveat in this area, even though you or your business buddy may not be able to do business with this person, they may be able to connect you to someone who can, so be discerning with your conversations.

Step 8   What Next? - How to Initiate a Follow Up Meeting

You've been speaking to this person now for a while and you think you may be able to sell them something or provide a service, how do you ask for the 'sale'? Short answer...You don't! Never try to sell anything at the first meeting, rather spend the time building trust, getting to know them and arranging to meet with them at a later date to discuss possibilities.

The conversation might go like this "It seems like you and I have a lot in common and I think we may be able to help each other in business, how about we have a coffee next week to explore how that might work?" Suggest a mutually suitable place to meet and lock in a time and date. Alternatively, you could do this after the function, though I like the idea of striking while the iron is hot and set a meeting while you are still fresh in their mind and they have good vibes about you.

Step 9   Follow Up - Do What You Promised

After the function, the first thing you must do is follow up. If you promised to do something…Do it! If you said you would send a report that you've read, then send the report. If you said you would follow up with a phone call to book a coffee meeting, then make the call. If you didn't promise anything, then I suggest you send every person you met a short hand-written note. How many hand-written notes do you receive these days? Not too many I would guess.

You can either have some purpose made stationery to write on or buy some nice postcards or greeting cards. Write a short note that says something like "Hi Nev, it was so nice to meet you this morning at the Business Breakfast, I look forward to getting to know you more in the future". Of course, there are many other variations and I'll cover them later.

Finally, connect on social media, if appropriate. My first port of call after a business function is LinkedIn, next it may be Facebook, Twitter, Instagram, etc. You decide from there how well you know the person or want to know the person and connect with them appropriately.

Step 10   Give Trust to Get Trust

The final step is to give trust, so that you get trust. What do I mean by this? Trust is the outcome of kept promises, so keep your promises, do what you said you would do. Next find a way to show you genuinely trust them. Perhaps you could call and ask for advice, you could send a testimonial on LinkedIn, you could praise them in a post on Twitter, or post on Facebook. Find a way to show you trust them and they in turn will return the trust to you.

Where to From Here?

Well, now you have the basics of how to get into relationships, let me expand on the model for you, so you can become an expert at this and use it to meet serious business connections and lever off those connections to secure some great business opportunities.

Relationship Building Action Steps

1. Review and ask yourself if handheld electronic devices interrupt or interfere with your ability to communicate effectively to others? If so maybe it's time to change how you manage the use of these devices.

2. Review how much time to spend communicating by electronic devices, when you could be talking face to face?

3. Ask Yourself:
   a. Are you afraid to talk to influential people?
   b. Are you afraid of rejection by others?
   c. Are you afraid you'll look silly, non-professional or amateurish?

4. What are your blocks that stop you building effective business relationships?

5. Read and implement the Relationship Guy Ten Step Model

Chapter 2

I Think I'll Build Our House

It was January 1992 when I came home and said to my wife Debby, "I think I'll build our house." You see we had our family home on the market and were looking to move up into a bigger house. The home we lived in was a modest three-bedroom, two-story home in Ferny Grove, a leafy suburb in Brisbane and an ideal location, close to schools, shops and the train station. The thing was we had outgrown it and wanted a little more space.

In those days, I worked in the Australian Taxation Office as a human resources consultant. We were about to move from the City to Chermside, an outer suburb on the North side of Brisbane into a purpose-built building designed especially for the decentralisation of the Taxation Office. The Tax Office had decided that it would break into three offices in Brisbane with roughly 600 staff in each office, one on the North side, one on the Southside and one in the City. I chose to go work on the North side.

That meant we could move into a house anywhere in an arc from where we currently lived in Ferny Grove, right around a broad swathe of suburbs to Chermside in the North. We looked at established houses and looked at vacant land.

Looking through the paper one morning, I saw an advertisement for acreage land for sale at Bunya, in the arc between Ferny Grove and Chermside. We had friends living on acreage and I loved the space. I thought, "We'll never be able to afford it, but what the hell, why not go have a look?" We drove out there on a Saturday morning, talked to the sales guy in his little humpy shed, got the price list and began exploring.

Guess what? We figured out we could afford the land after all and just three days later we put a deposit on a block of land, just $20,000 over our budget! It was the perfect block for us though, had just the right number of trees, a natural break in the middle for a house site and was well and truly above any possible worst-case flood possibilities. This was critical as we had both lived through the worst flood in Brisbane's history in 1974 and were very conscious of any possible flooding challenges.

The land was 6,000 square metres or one and a half acres, with plenty of room to move and a natural oval in what would be our back yard for the kids to play in. Once we secured the land we had to sell our property at Ferny Grove before we could begin construction.

Fast forward a few months later and we had been looking at house designs and figuring out what it might cost to hire a builder to build a house.

"I think I'll build our house," I said. Debby didn't say much. "It can't be that hard. Paul and I have been talking about it at work". Paul, was Paul Carney a fellow human resources consultant and good friend from the Tax Office. He had just bought five acres of land at Ocean View, about 45 minutes north from where we had just purchased. He was going to build his house and basically, we talked each other into doing it.

It became a reality when we went to the bank and asked our friendly Bank Manager if he would lend us the money. As we owned the previous house and were soon to be cashed up from the sale he didn't hesitate to say: "Yes!"

Consequently, I started buying How to Build a House books from the bookstores and think about how I might achieve this.

One thing I knew was that my relationship networks were sound and I was sure that I could find good trades people to do what I needed to do. If I just worked my relationships, I was sure I would be fine.

I started with my oldest brother Neville, he's a civil design draftsman, so understands building design. He said, "You want a house plan drawn, I know just the guy for you". My eldest brother Neville is one of the best relationship management people I know. He knows everyone and stays in touch with them as well. He is the best "keep-in-toucher" person I know. Yes, keeper-in-toucher, a technical term! Over the years, he has worked all over Queensland and the Northern Territory. He has met some interesting people and no matter what, he establishes a relationship with them. Perhaps he may not like them all, however he does know whom to contact when someone needs something. He definitely has the relationship DNA.

We met with Dave the house designer and told him what we wanted.

"I want a low set, long straight house," I said. "I want to be able to drive into my garage and get the sleeping kids out of the car and step into the house and put them into bed". At the time, it was the fashion on acreage blocks to build a separate garage next to the house and have it connected to the house by a walkway or similar.

It wasn't just about the kids, though that was important, as they were just seven and five years old at the time. It was as much about building the house that I requested a single storey, straight house, it would be easier to build!

So, a week or so later the designer calls and says, "I have the first draft of your plans in the post, let me know what you think." We ripped open the envelope to see a boomerang shaped house, nothing like the long, straight house I ordered. All I could think of was the drama in building a house with a bend in the middle. I picked up the phone "What happened to the long, straight house?"

"Well" he says, "you did say you wanted to drive straight into your garage and take your sleeping kids from the car and put them to bed correct?"

Well, he got that right.

"So, I had to put the garage in the middle of the house and angle a wing off each side to make this work, so you step into your family room. If I gave you a long, straight house, you would have to put the garage on either end. This would mean that you would drive in and step out of the garage, either into your main bedroom or your formal lounge. Which would you prefer?" He asked. I pondered this for a moment "The boomerang shape is looking good" I replied.

The first test was over, we had a plan, now I had to begin the project in earnest and find a long list of tradesmen and suppliers.

Connecting in the Business World

When you are thinking of connecting in the business world, it's a very similar process. Start out by thinking 'who do I know?' Start writing their names down and make a comprehensive list. Better still go to your phone and check out your list of contacts. I guarantee that when you scroll through the list you will find names of people there that you have forgotten you even knew! I regularly just scroll through my contacts and connect with people I haven't spoken to in some time.

Clever relationship management specialists have already graded their contacts into categories. A typical grading system might be A, B and C contacts. 'A' contacts are those you do business with regularly or perhaps those that refer business to you regularly. These are the people that you want to keep in touch with regularly, because they bring you good things. Every thirty days is a good time frame to reconnect with these people.

'B' contacts are the people that you do business with perhaps a few times a year, or again maybe they refer you business a few times a year to you. These people are still good connections and are worthy of some form of contact from you every sixty days.

The 'C' connections are the rest of your contacts. These are people that you've met, probably have done one piece of business with, or perhaps they have referred some business to you once. Maybe you have just met them at a business function and you think you may be able to do business with them at some stage, so keeping in touch is a good strategy. In past years, I have done a lot of work in the Credit Union industry with emerging leaders. I have kept a record of all the participants on my programs and still keep in touch. My theory is that one day they will get promoted and remember me fondly and when they have the authority and the budget, they will hire me to work for their organisation.

It's a long-range strategy, however it has already paid dividends for me over time just by keeping in touch.

Think about the people you want to meet, or the kind of people you want to meet and hopefully do business with. Never be afraid to make a list of people you haven't yet met. If you know they could be the perfect client for you write their name down. Someone else on your list will most likely know them and will be only too willing to introduce you.

When I started making a list of trades people I knew and the trades I needed, there were some gaping holes. However, I quickly found that by using the simple question, "Who do you know who?" led me to fill the gaps in my list.

My neighbour Rob, from across the road was a handyman, all-rounder type of guy, very capable with his hands without necessarily having a trade qualification. When I showed him my list he quickly helped me find the perfect concreter to pour the slab for the house, one of the gaps on my list.

Three Kinds of Connections

There are three kinds of connections in the business world and if you think about it, you will certainly know people in each of these categories. The three categories are, Gurus, Greats and Go To's.

Gurus

The Guru connections are the people that you go to for the facts, the inside view or the details that you don't have and wish you did. These people are usually experienced business people in a certain industry or vocation. They aren't necessarily university professors or learned scholars, they are more well-connected people within their industry or niche, they know lots and they also know lots of people. If you ask a question and they personally don't know the answer, they will surely know the person that does know the answer.

Here are some typical gurus:

- People from your profession or your professional association.
- People just like you, often they work in the same industry or profession.
- Blog writers, authors in general, online experts in a specific topic.
- Consultants, trainers or coaches related to a specific industry.

- Retired colleagues from your business or industry.
- Your close business associates and even your competitors.

Gurus are all around, you simply have to keep your eyes open to identify the right person at the right time for you.

Greats

My professional body is Professional Speakers Australia. In that organisation I am surrounded by some of the Greats of the industry. Many of these people are readily approachable to offer support, advice or direction when I am lost or unsure. In fact, when I joined the Association, one of the senior members of my local Chapter took me under his wing and became my mentor, my personal sounding board as I started and then built my business. Today he and I are good mates, he is still a "Great" and I can still call on him to support me, with help, advice or direction if necessary.

Greats are often there for you in through thick and thin, they become your personal cheer squad, they cheer for you when you have a success and they pick you up and dust you off when you've had a catastrophic failure, or simply stumbled along the way.

Here are some typical Greats:

- Your mentor or perhaps your coach.
- Your colleagues or friends in your profession or professional association.
- Your best friends, your partner and or your family. No one supports you better than a loved one, a family member.
- Members of your church, a sporting club or even a social club.
- People that you've worked with in the past; colleagues, managers or supervisors.
- People that you may have mentored or coached.

Go To's

Go To connections are the people that are well connected. They have relationships with many people and they are constantly doing business with those people, based on those strong relationships. These people are the connectors in business and often introduce others into their inner circle to do business with their trusted connections. The interesting part here is that Go To connectors may also perform the role of Guru or Great for you as well. They can become the font of all knowledge, because of their extensive experience and because of their extensive connections.

Go To's are relationship magnets and attract similar kinds of people, they are often surrounded by quality business people. Others look on and wonder how they have so many connections and often ask "How can I be like you?"

Here are some typical Go To's:

- Clients that have worked with the Go To for many years.
- People that have referred business to you.
- People that you have referred business to.
- People in your mastermind group.
- People in your Chamber of Commerce, your professional Association or your business network group.
- Your Referral Circle - people that you share the same target market with, though they don't compete with you.

Once you understand who is in your network, you can go to them selectively, for just the right situation. Take a moment now and make a list of who is in your network. Which category do they fit into?

Relationship Building Action Steps

1. Review your database and remind yourself just who you are connected with.

2. Maybe it's time to weed out old contacts that you no longer are really connected with.

3. Identify you're A, B & C Clients in your list.

4. Design a contact strategy for the A, B & C Clients on your list.

5. Identify who are your Gurus

6. Identify who are you Greats

7. Identify who are your Go To's

8. It's OK to be selective here, only choose a maximum of ten or less for each category. Once you have decided, then devise a connection strategy to capitalize on your relationship.

Chapter 3

Activate Your Network

I thought, if I'm going to build a house I better get started.

I started to make a list. Interestingly my list wasn't so much a list of building materials, more a list of people I knew. I was thinking that the best way to do this was to approach people I knew, or people who were recommended to me by people I knew and trusted. So that became my modus operandi, find people I knew who could help me build a house.

It's amazing what happens when you spread the word, when you activate your relationships and connections and ask for help. Help arrives in the most amazing ways at times and certainly from unexpected quarters.

In a famous poem written by Henry Wadsworth Longfellow entitled "Midnight Ride" he tells the story of Paul Revere and his actions on the evening of 18 April 1775. In the poem, Revere prepares to alert his countrymen about an attack by the British in Boston by land or by sea. The legend goes that once he discovers the attack will be by sea, he rides throughout Middlesex County to alert his countrymen to rise to arms and protect their country. Two other riders join him and they spread the word far and wide.

The poem is apparently riddled with inaccuracies; however, the point is that he activated his relationships and spread the word far and wide and his fellow countrymen rose to support him.

The first lesson to learn about relationships is that we have them all around us and sometimes we simply need to alert people to the fact that we need help. If you have a good relationship, then people will step up to help assist and guide you.

Once I activated my network it was amazing what happened next; people seemed enthused by the project and got on board with offers of help or guidance.

My children were only little at this stage, my son was still in kindergarten (kindy), my daughter was at school. One of my son Drew's best play mates at kindy was Bernie. Bernie was not as you might expect, another boy, in fact a girl called Bernadette, well Drew called her Bernie.

I was elected to the Board of Management of the kindergarten Association and attended meetings regularly to manage the Association's business. I went along one night to one of these meetings and bumped into Bernie's Dad, he was known as "Moose". Don't ask me how he got this name, because I don't really know, though he was a big Moose of a man!

After the meeting, we are having a cup of tea and Moose sidles up to me and says, "I hear you are building a house?" "Yep, that's correct," I respond. "What type of roof are you fitting?" was the next question. "Corrugated iron, of course" I responded, corrugated iron being a very popular building material at the time. "Good", he said, "When you are ready let me know and I'll sort it for you". I looked at him kind of puzzled, you see I didn't really know what Moose did for a living. He caught my confused look and then said, "I deliver roofing iron for a living". Now it all made sense.

Moose was good to his word, the roof cost me just half of what it would have if I had ordered it through a "normal" supplier. He saved me just over $7,000, now that's a lot of money.

How Do You Activate Your Network?

Activating your network can be as simple as telling just one person what you need and asking if they know someone who can assist you. I have often just slipped my need into general conversation asking the age-old question..."Who do you know who?"

It might work like this. I want to redesign my business cards and so need a graphic designer. The person I used last time was too expensive and unresponsive so I want to get a recommendation for someone new.

This would be my typical approach. I would contact my network in the following order and ask "I need some new business cards. Who do you know who is a good graphic designer?"

Mastermind Group

My first port of call would be my inner circle, the people I go to for help and support typically, my Greats. I would get on the phone and ask who they have used and who would they recommend. The members of my mastermind group are business people like me, people who I trust and rely. This is the simplest way to activate your network, start close by and work out from there.

The Key 4

After my inner circle, the people I go to for help and support typically are my Key 4. My Key 4 are four other business people that I have carefully chosen to work closely with, they support me and I support them in business. We all share the same target market; however, we do not compete with each other. I'll talk in more detail about the

Key 4 later in the book. Suffice to say, these people are my closest business allies.

I would get on the phone to my Key 4 and ask who they have used and who would they recommend. This is the simplest way to activate your network. As I have said: Start close by and work out from there.

Your Social Networks

Assuming I have no success with my Key 4 group I would go wider next and call in my larger network: Social Media. I'm active on Facebook, LinkedIn and Twitter predominately, so I would likely post there. I might say something like..."Who do you know who is a great graphic designer? I'll need new business cards and I'm looking for recommendations for a graphic designer, one who is not too expensive and responsive to my requests."

A post like this would activate a huge response I suspect, as I have large networks across these three platforms. Perhaps I may wish to limit the responses and just post to a select group across those platforms or maybe I could just choose one social media platform, like Facebook. Either way, once I post, my network would respond.

Your Blog

I could write a blog about my experiences with previous graphic designers and ask my blog readers to come back to me with suggestions. You get the idea.

If you have steadily worked at building your relationships in the past, then activating your network should not be a real problem. Remember the more relationships you have, the larger the network you have and the larger the reach you have when you need to connect with someone. I'll talk more later about how to connect with just the right person for you, or perhaps to meet the best possible prospect for your business.

Relationship Building Action Steps

1. Focus on what you want/need, then activate your network. Ask the question "Who do you know who..."

2. Summon the help of your Mastermind Group or Key 4 to access who or what you need.

3. If you don't have a Mastermind Group or Key 4, identify four other like-minded business people that share your target market, yet don't compete with you. Invite them to meet with you on a regular basis to enhance your relationships and grow your business.

Chapter 4

You Meet Someone at a Function

If you are like me, you attend a lot of business functions and networking events. I've found over the years that attending functions is a great way to meet new people, keep in touch with old friends and learn new information. I attend some functions regularly every month and others just every now and then. Of course, there are some events that only happen once a year, so whilst they are in my calendar, it is not a huge commitment to keep up with attendance.

One of the most amazing things I have noticed at functions is just how poorly people deal with meeting strangers. People are very good at the basics, which go something like this. You meet someone new and typically you would shake hands and introduce yourself saying your name.

"Hello, my name is David Stephenson"

The next most often repeated phrase after this one is, "Tell me, what do you do?"

This will be met with many and varied responses and realistically there is a science around what to say next. Having said that, here's a typical response and by the way, this is a transcript of a real conversation, only the names have been changed to protect the innocent!

"I'm a scientist, however I didn't really like the laboratory work, too much politics, so I got out of science and I'm now working for a Government Agency in their IT department. I spend a lot of time with ill-mannered people telling them how to restart their computer to fix really simple problems!"

How would you respond to this person? This response is what I would call a conversation closer, it causes the conversation to shut down. After hearing that response, I'm not sure I want to hear much more from this clearly cynical person and their adventures with their "ill mannered" clients.

Here's the response given by someone in the group:

"Oh, that's interesting", followed quickly by the person who initiated the question turning at a forty-five-degree angle away from the IT dude to someone else in the group and saying, "Geoffrey, so nice to see you again, how's business?"

What followed next was a lively conversation between Geoffrey and our protagonist about Geoffrey's business adventures, while the IT guy was politely ignored.

Then there's always the shorter version:

"Hello, my name is David Stephenson"

"Tell me, what do you do?"

"I work in IT"

Can you see where I'm going here?

My belief is that the majority of people attending business functions are poor at establishing and maintaining relationships. They simply don't know what to say after hello in order to take the relationship further. Often after the "Tell me what you do?" question is answered, there are 'crickets'. That is a deathly silence while the annoying sound of crickets chirping in the background fills the room.

I'm sure this never happens to you, however, if it does, read on. I have the solution for you in the following chapters.

Relationship Building Action Steps

1. Practice how you respond when someone asks, "What do you do?"

2. Think of a response that will open up the conversation, rather than closing it down.

Chapter 5

Listen More, Talk Less

When you are talking to another person for the first or even the twenty-first time, you must give them one hundred percent of your attention, concentrating solely on what they are saying or doing. Listen more, talk less. If you want to get into relationship quickly, you must show the other person that you are interested in them. Listen more, talk less. The best way to show interest is to listen carefully to what they are saying, hang on their every word, ask questions that reinforce what they are saying or allow them to talk more about the topic they are addressing. Listen more, talk less!

I can't tell you the number of times I've attended a function and met someone for the first time and then noticed as we engaged in conversation that they are busy scanning the room over my shoulder, looking to see who else is in the room that they may want to connect with. Clearly, they are not really interested in me or building a solid or valued relationship with me.

Being there is about focus, focusing on the person or persons in front of you, making them the centre of your attention for at least the next three to five minutes of your entire life. It may sound a little dramatic, however it works. The person you are engaging will notice that you are there for them and no one else.

What do you do if there is more than one person, it's not that complicated, focus on the conversation? Listen to the words, think about what is being said, find a way to add value to the conversation, perhaps ask a question to explore the topic further.

Listen More, Talk Less!

Before I took long service leave to work on the house, I had to fly to Canberra, our nation's capital for work. It was the Monday of a long weekend and the plane was nearly empty. When I boarded, the flight attendant said sit where you like, we don't mind. I sat beside this guy who looked friendly and started a conversation. It turns out we had a lot in common. The conversation went something like this. "Hi, I'm Lindsay Adams", he then introduced himself. I asked the usual question, "So what do you do?" He responded, "I'm the State Sales Manager for Austral Bricks". "Bricks" I said, my eyes lighting up, "I'm building a house at the moment, I could use some bricks". We both laughed and started talking about my home building project. He was quite surprised to hear that I was planning to build a house myself, even though I had no building experience. I went on to tell him about my plans, the style of house, the location and my progress to date.

By the end of the plane ride we were almost old friends, we had joked and laughed and talked about the dangers and pitfalls of building a house. We finally landed in Canberra and as he got his bag out of the overhead locker, he passed me his business card. "When you're ready to start that house, give me a call," he said. "I'll be sure look after you with some really nice bricks". I was a little taken aback, and yet thrilled at the same time.

A few weeks later I followed up and gave him a call to see if he was serious about his offer. In between I had done my homework and looked at his range of bricks and figured out what we could afford. My wife and I had chosen a mid-range brick, which fitted our budget at the time. When I rang, I received a gracious reception and an enthusiastic invitation to come visit him at his sales office. We arrived at the appointed time and were shown into his office by his assistant.

We did the usual small talk and then got down to business, I showed him the brick we had chosen and our budget. He looked horrified, "You don't want that brick" he said. "This is the brick you need," he said pointing to the most expensive brick in the range.

"The problem with that brick is the price," I said, "it's way outside our budget".

Here's where the conversation got interesting.... "Don't worry about that" he says, "I told you I would look after you".

An hour later we left his office having just purchased 12,000 bricks. Boy, did he look after us; he gave us an amazing price. The price was so low that when I told my bricklayer, he wouldn't believe me. Apparently even the bricklayer couldn't buy the bricks at that price and he regularly bought from this company.

Who knew this little encounter would turn into 12,000 bricks. Maybe your next chance encounter could turn into 12,000 bricks or even better 12,000 bars of gold for you. Listen more, talk less.

The Hand Shake

One of the first things that will usually happen when you meet someone new is that you will shake hands with the other person as you greet them and say your name. Let's focus on the handshake first.

As you meet more and more people you will begin to understand that not everyone shakes hands like you do. When I was growing up my Dad taught me to shake hands firmly with the other person and look them directly in the eye and say your name clearly.

This method works with most people and fits a lot of cultures around the world. The key when shaking hands is to try to match the other person, be like them. Not always easy when you've only just met. When you clasp hands, try to match the pressure as they are clasping your hand. I've had some bone crusher handshakes in my time, which are just not an enjoyable experience. If you aren't sure err on the side of a gentler handshake rather than crush the other person's hand.

When you hold out your hand, aim to get the web between the thumb and forefinger of the other person's hand snuggly fitting against the web of your hand. Clasp your fingers around their hand and gently squeeze, enough that you have a firm grip, without squeezing the life out of their hand! At the same time look the person you are greeting in the eye, engage them in a sincere gaze, let them know by your look, that you are interested to meet them.

Often when I meet people and shake their hand they look at the ground, over my shoulder, out the window...whatever. What they are telling me is that they aren't really interested in meeting or engaging with me at all, they are simply going through the motions. Let your new friend know you are interested in them, shake their hand, greet them warmly.

You can learn a lot about other people just by their handshake and this will assist you to build relationships quicker. Suffice to say, you can tell a lot about the other person simply by shaking hands. The humble handshake can help you direct conversation, ask the right questions and even close a sale.

Be aware that in different cultures, you may have a different hand shake experience. In Asia, handshakes are not always as firm as you may experience in other cultures. They can sometimes be described as the "wet fish" handshake. They are very gentle and are more a simple clasp of each other's hands, rather than a firm grip, which we may be more used to in the western world.

A small word on shaking hands with women. Once upon a time men never shook hands with women, a very long time ago in fact. Today it is acceptable in most modern societies to shake hands with women of all ages at business functions and private events. A simple trick I learned many years ago was wait for the woman to extend her hand, if she did, shake it. It's not rocket science.

There are still some cultures around the world where women do not shake hands. In these cultures, women do not offer their hand to shake. Again, be there, watch what is going on and understand the situation.

The next part of the handshake is the exchange of names.

The Importance of Names

During the initial greeting phase, you will tell the other person your name and of course, they will tell you theirs. Listen carefully! A person's name is very important to them, make sure you get it right. A typical engagement might go like this "Hello, I'm Lindsay Adams," "Hello I'm Dixie Carlton, nice to meet you".

The next sentence I use will include the person's name again, so that I can cement their name into my brain. "Lovely to meet you too, Dixie, what do you do?"

Alternately, "Lovely to meet you Dixie, tell me about your business". I am going to use their name and ask an open-ended question to get them speaking about themselves.

An interesting fact, if you engage in conversation with someone and get them talking mostly about themselves rather than you, they will leave the conversation with you thinking that you are such a nice person. Why is that? Because they got to talk about themselves in the conversation. Simple yet true, so get people talking about themselves, rather than you.

Follow the 80/20 rule here, get them talking about themselves around eighty percent of the time and talking about you, just twenty percent of the time. It works.

Use their name often in the conversation, when you repeat their name it is like music to their ears. Make sure you get their name right and pronounce it correctly, getting it wrong will grate every time you say it.

If you aren't good at remembering names there is a couple of things you can do to help. Keep their business card handy so you can refer to it. If I'm in a meeting with a prospect or client for the first time, I will leave their business card on the table in front of me, so I can easily refer to it. If I'm at a stand-up function, I may hold their card in my hand for a few minutes and glance at it occasionally to refresh my memory.

Relationship Building Action Steps

1. Ask yourself, Am I a good listener?

    a. Do I need to listen more, talk less?
    b. Focus on the other person 100%, listen to every word
        they say, as if it's the most important conversation of the
        day.

2. Review your handshake:

    a. Do you grip the other person's hand web to web?
    b. Make sure you match pressure, avoid squeezing too hard.
    c. Make eye contact.
    d. Smile.
    e. When it is culturally appropriate, offer your hand to a
        woman to shake.

3. Listen carefully for other people's names and use them in your
    conversation.

4. Keep their business card handy in case you can't easily
    remember their name.

5. Apply the 80/20 rule to the conversation. Get them speaking
    80 % of the time, you speak 20% of the time.

Chapter 6

Swap Business Cards

There comes a point in the interaction when you will decide it's time to swap business cards. In Australia, exchanging business cards can be a haphazard operation. I've seen many people at different functions going around the room quickly meeting people, saying hello; then exchanging business cards. Worse still, I attended a breakfast networking function where I saw a woman go to each place at every table and leave a flyer and her business card. She then raced around the room shaking hands and introducing herself to as many people as possible.

I watched carefully at the end of the breakfast to see what happened to her business cards and flyers, sure enough most them were left behind or pushed onto side tables. But wait, it gets worse! About three hours later, I received an email from her offering to sell me something, her magnificent special of the month or whatever. That email was quickly reassigned to my email blacklist.

The problem is, she didn't make any attempt to create a relationship with me, so there is no chance I will do business with her based on the simple exchange of a business card.

I've done a lot of work in Asia, having worked there since 2004. In Asia, there is a protocol around exchanging business cards and whilst it can be a little intimidating for first time western visitors, I have adopted part of their process when I exchange business cards with anyone, anywhere.

In Asia, the business card is always offered to the other party held between the thumb and forefinger of both hands together. That is a two-handed exchange. It can be awkward when both parties offer their card at the same moment. One party must break the impasse and take the others card.

Once this happens, both parties read each other's card like it is the best novel they have read in the longest time. I like this part of the exchange and do this regularly as a matter of course now with anyone's card, no matter what country I'm visiting. I honour their card and want them to understand that I've read it, I like it and I'm interested in them as a business person.

I always read the card and then make a deliberate comment about the card. I might comment on the photo, if there is one, perhaps the font, their slogan or if nothing else the locations of their office. "I see you are based in Brunswick Street, that's such an interesting area", I might say.

I am being there for them, by reading their card. I've seen many people exchange cards at events where they basically take a cursory glance and put the card into their top pocket, or somewhere never to be seen again.

I use the business card as a ready reminder of the person I have met and I always make notes on the business card to remind me about the person, what we talked about, what I promised to send them or even whether they are a good prospect for me and then what they may be interested in buying from me. The tricky part here is not to let the other person see you taking notes on their card.

In Asia, this is a big no-no, it's not acceptable to write on someone's business card especially in front of them. It's a sign of disrespect. I have in the past resorted to clandestine scribbling or I quickly excuse myself from a conversation to perhaps freshen my drink, to quickly scribble a note or two on the back of someone's card so that I remember what I need from the interaction.

In Australia, it's a lot more laid back, however I still take the respectful route and often will ask the other person if they mind me writing on their card. The response is very often, "Sure, no problem at all". "Go your hardest!"

What to Do with the Cards

I have perfected a system for handling business cards and I recommend that you think carefully about where you keep your cards and how you deal with other peoples' cards. I keep all my business cards in my left suit pocket. I'm right handed so it's easy to reach in and quickly produce a card for someone I'm speaking with. Once I receive a card I inspect it carefully, make a relevant comment and if I'm standing I'll then file the card in my right suit pocket. This keeps the two groups of cards separated and does not allow for confusion.

I've met many people that have reached into their pocket and offered me a card which clearly does not belong to them. They didn't have a system and got all the cards they collected, plus their own mixed up in their pocket. Ladies can use their handbags and have a separate space to store their own cards and then the new cards they collect.

If I'm not wearing a coat, I usually have a business card holder in my left trouser pocket and again store the cards I've collected in my right trouser pocket. It doesn't matter where you put them, just make sure you know where you keep yours and theirs and make sure they never meet in the middle.

Once I get back to my office, I go through the cards and sort them. I sort them into three piles: immediate action, or possible business, potential business or referrals and finally, nice to have met and good to be polite and demonstrate the true Relationships Guy approach. That is, you can never have too many people in your network and if you are polite and friendly, it will reflect positively on your brand and reputation.

Once I've sorted the cards, I take whatever action is necessary to deal with each of the groups. If it is a potential sale, I may send a proposal or prepare more information for a meeting. If it is a potential business contact I may send them more information to consider or perhaps speak to someone I know and trust who knows this same person to discuss a strategic referral approach.

Finally, the balance and in fact all the cards will get a hand-written note, saying how nice it was to meet them.

Once this is done, I will enter the cards into my database with a note identifying where I met the owner and any other pertinent information for the future. I may also enrol them into my regular newsletter, podcast or sales system promoting one of my online learning programs.

Stories

As I was writing this chapter, I was sitting on a plane travelling from Brisbane to Los Angeles and I bumped into two old business friends on the plane. I made a point of going to the seat they were sitting in and began catching up. It had been some time since we have seen each other and of course there were stories to tell.

This couple is interesting she owns a residential real estate agency and he is a graphic designer, specializing in website design. We ended up standing outside the toilets and talking, each telling stories about what we've been up to, how our children were and where we were flying to.

I am reminded again about the power of listening more and talking less and focusing on them 100%. Each of us had a story to tell and each of us listened intently as the story unfolded. Storytelling is such a classic way of getting and holding people's attention.

How many times have you been talking with someone at a function and they are rabbiting on about something or other which is about as exciting as watching paint dry?

The challenge here is to find the essence of their story. Which part is of value to you? You could stand there and pretend that the story is interesting, politely nodding or smiling at the prompts, or you could actively listen to distil what's in this for both of us here.

Think of it this way. I am listening to you out of respect and I'm trying hard to be interested. I am determined to listen so that I can get a better insight into you, the person with whom I want to do business. There is a piece of gold here for me somewhere, a piece of understanding about your behaviour, values or decision-making process.

Not every story is riveting and some people have the happy knack of crucifying every story they tell. Never the less, there is still learning to take place...focus on them 100%

A couple of simple tips about storytelling. Focus on the other person 100%. If you are the storyteller, be there as you tell the story, that is relive the moment. Feel the shivers creep up your spine, see the vivid picture as you describe it, involve your audience whether they're number one or one hundred.

If you are the listener, be there. Put yourself in the other person's shoes, feel the fear, hear the noise, or see the amazing scene unfold.

The more you 'be there', the more you are with the other person, the more they are with you...in relationship.

Jokes

Telling jokes is a spectacular way to get into a relationship with people and a spectacular way to get out of a relationship. The art of joke telling has largely died. I believe mainly due to the advent of the Internet. Once upon a time jokes were largely passed by word of mouth. Some people are just good joke tellers and others aren't, everyone has a cross to bear.

Before email was common, jokes were told by those who were skilled joke tellers at business events, or over the phone, or by one to one conversation. Some people were acknowledged good joke tellers and always had a joke, which may or may not have been appropriate depending on the situation.

Jokes were generally passed from function to function and had use by dates based on current affairs.

Today jokes are passed quickly around the world based on current affairs via email, joke websites and social media. What once relied on the quick wit and delivery style of the office comic has now been superseded by written humour, distributed at the click of a button.

If you are at a business function and someone is telling a joke, there are some relationship rules to consider.

Rule number 1: Be there, focus 100% on them. Listen carefully as the joke teller builds to the punch line, laugh out loudly and joyfully as the punch line is delivered. Because of the nature of joke telling, there is a chance you have heard the joke before, that's OK, be there, let the joke teller share the punch line.

Rule number 2: Never, ever steal their thunder and say the punch line before they do. Listen carefully, maybe they tell it better than you, maybe they don't, remember there's learning in this for both of you and there's a relationship in there for both of you as well.

Imagine how the joke teller would feel if you stole their golden punch line, or you deflate their joke by saying, "Oh that old one, I've heard that before".

Rule number 3: Even if you've heard it a hundred times before, be there for the joke teller, listen and laugh.

Real Conversations Create Real Relationships

If you are serious about building relationships quickly with people, you must pay careful attention to your conversation skills. Listening intently is a good way to deepen a relationship quickly. In fact, I would again suggest that you listen more and speak less. No great relationship was ever created by one person proving to another how much they know!

Step back from your urge to impress for a moment and consider these three strategies to grow your relationships at business functions.

1.   Review your conversation techniques

When you are speaking to another person are you learning more about them and sharing about yourself? Asking another person about themselves is the simplest way to get a conversation going and the more you ask the quicker your relationship deepens.

Does the conversation reflect your views and opinions, and does it help to focus your views? Having an opinion is one thing, being willing to share your view and learn from others' knowledge and opinions to broaden or develop your own is the key here. Always be willing to learn from others.

Do you feel moved, ready to take action or simply satisfied with the information you are sharing? Getting involved in a conversation that engages your emotions is a powerful way to connect. Feeling moved or ready to take action means you have connected at a deeper level and understood the core message. Imagine if you could leave every conversation having moved others to take action.

2.   Turn Every Conversation into Give and Take

Often when we are at a business function we want to get our message across, tell people what we do, figure out if they are a potential prospect or client and share lots of good information about our product or service.

Just stop for a moment and consider what might happen if you were to make every conversation about give and take. So, give first. Ask the other person what they do, ask them how they do that, how their product or service is delivered. Think about whether this is something you may find useful or perhaps if you know anyone who may be interested in their product?

This is true giving.

The time to talk will appear soon enough. Start first with giving, put the urge to wax lyrical about what you do on hold and genuinely listen to what the other person is saying. I can almost guarantee that if you listen and ask the other person about themselves first, they will then turn the conversation around and ask about you.

This is the give and take process. At this point and at only this point do you begin to talk about what you do and how you may be able to help the other person or perhaps someone they know.

3.   Listen Actively, Respond Sparingly

People know when you are listening or just pretending to listen. You can tell if another person is listening to you by their body language, their posture, their eyes. Remember if you can tell that someone's not listening to you, it works both ways.

Practice active listening techniques. Engage the other person fully with your eyes, look at their face as they speak, watch their lips move, notice the angle of their head, watch their gestures. As they speak give them visual and verbal cues that you are paying attention, nod your head in agreement, use following phrases like "Wow, okay, that's interesting". Using short phrases like this lets them know that you are following what they are saying. Respond using thoughtful open-ended questions, which will enable them to elaborate more and give you a full and complete explanation.

Remember real relationships are based on real conversations.

By taking a proactive approach to the art of good conversations, you can quickly deepen your relationships. Never be afraid to be passionate about your subject and allow and encourage those you are engaging to show their passion. Listen carefully and ask questions that show you are listening. Remember to give and take in the conversation with the aim of giving first. Add these together and you will be a master of conversation and relationships.

Relationship Building Action Steps

1. Exchange business cards only after you have had a meaningful conversation.

2. Once you receive their card, read it like it's the best blockbuster, thriller novel!

3. Make some positive comment about their card.

4. Develop a system for your business cards:

   a. Where do you keep your cards?
   b. Where do you put their cards?

5. If you tell a joke, make it appropriate for the group. Never tell a joke about anyone in the room, it may offend them, the best jokes are self-deprecating.

Chapter 7

Ask Clever Questions

The Plumbing Rep Drove in Unannounced off the Street

Dad and I were up on the roof one day, standing roof trusses, when a car drove into the site. We didn't recognise the car, so were kind of wondering who this might be. A tall guy with neatly styled hair climbed out of the vehicle and says, "I'm looking for the owner". "You found him" I responded.

He introduced himself as Steve Owens; he was a representative with one of the large plumbing supply companies based nearby. Now this was almost a long-distance conversation as I was standing up on the top of the wall frame and he was on the ground, well below my feet.

The conversation went something like this:

Steve: "So, you're the owner?"
Me: "Yes that's right"
Steve: "And you're building this house on your own?"
Me: "Well not completely alone, I have my Dad here helping out!"
Steve: "So you're a carpenter then?"
Me: "No, not really. I'm a public servant on long service leave, I just decided I wanted to build my own house".

Steve: "So is your Dad a carpenter then?"

Me: "Nope, he's my Dad. He's pretty handy with the tools though".

Steve: "So you're telling me that you're a public servant. Which Department do you work for?"

Me: "I work for the Australian Taxation Office".

Steve: "So you work for the Tax Office and you're building your own house?"

Me: "Yep".

Steve: "Well I'm amazed. How did you know what to do, building a house is not a simple project?"

Me: "Well, I read a few books and I have a few friends that are helping out, it can't be that hard, can it?"

Steve: "Well, with an attitude like that, I guess not".

We went back and forth like this for quite a while, Steve asking me more questions, me answering them and I suspect for every honest answer I gave I could tell he was growing more and more impressed with what he was hearing.

Eventually I climbed down off the roof, we shook hands and talked all manner of stuff relating to owner building a house and having absolutely no prior experience as a house builder. Finally, he steered the conversation around to the purpose of his visit.

Steve: "Well, I'm very impressed, do you have any quotes on your plumbing supplies yet?"

Me: "As a matter of fact I do."

Steve: "Can I give you a quote as well?"

Me: "You better sharpen your pencil as I'm in the habit of receiving red hot quotes from people who want to do business with me."

Steve: "Can you give me a list of what you need?"

Me: "Sure can, I'll email it to you tonight if you like."

Steve: "That would be great and I will absolutely do my best for you."

Me: (Proffering my hand for him to shake) "Great, I look forward to the best quote possible."

With that we bid each other farewell and he got back into his car and drove off. Sure enough around one week later Steve came in with the best-priced quote I had received. Again, I compared notes with my plumber and he just shook his head when he saw the prices. "Lindsay, how do you do this he says?"

Asking Clever Questions

Asking Clever Questions is probably one of the best ways to be there for someone you want to build a relationship with. Let's go right back to the start here. We've shaken hands, we've identified what we do, our job, career, or role at this function. The next step is to begin asking Clever Questions.

Clever Questions are usually those that elicit a longer explanation, they usually come from open-ended questions rather than closed questions. A closed question is one that gets a yes/no response. They work for certain situations, however if you are trying to establish a relationship they tend to shut down conversations, so aim to ask questions that are more open ended.

Not sure what to ask? Here are some ideas. I've broken the questions into six categories. You can't possibly ask all these questions in one sitting and of course the whole idea is to ask a few well-placed questions to get the other person talking so you can discover what you have in common. Remember: focus on the other person and their business and listen.

The Five Clever Question Categories:

1. You
2. Your Business
3. Marketing
4. Social Media
5. Leadership

1.   You

1.   How did you happen to come to this event?
2.   What made you decide to attend?
3.   How did you find out about this function, how long have you been attending?
4.   What market are you in, who is your ideal client base?
5.   Have you ever had one of those days, or a client who just stands out?
6.   What would you do differently if you started all over again?
7.   Do you have children? How many? How old?
8.   Do you have any hobbies, interests, or a sport you are passionate about?
9.   What sporting team do you follow?
10. Are you a member of a professional association?

2.   Your Business

1.   Tell me about your business?
2.   What is the favourite part of your business?
3.   Who are your typical clients?
4.   How did you get into this line of work?
5.   What is the most common misunderstanding about your business?
6.   What makes your business different from others like yours?
7.   Tell me about some of the unique aspects to your business?
8.   What are some of the changes you've seen in your industry recently?
9.   What are some business magazines you would recommend?
10. What are some of the biggest challenges?
     a. Financial challenges
     b. Leadership challenges
     c. People challenges
     d. Business challenges etc. you've had?

3.   Marketing

1. What business books have you read recently that you've found valuable?
2. What are some of the marketing tactics that you've employed that have helped your business?
3. What are some of the biggest marketing challenges you've had?
4. How do you maintain contact with your clients or customers?
5. What are some of the ways you entertain your clients or customers?
6. What business events or groups have you found effective? Why? How?
7. What business events or groups have you found to be ineffective? Why? How?
8. What's the biggest block to selling/marketing in your business?
9. What are some of the ways you've overcome them?
10. What do you think motivates your prospects or customers to buy from you?

4.   Social Media

1. Which social media sites do you use? Do you have a company profile?
2. What are some business blogs or newsletters that pertain to your field?
3. What are some business blogs or newsletters you've read that you would recommend?
4. Have you ever used blogging or commenting on blogs as a business tool?
5. What do you think about blogging?
6. What are some websites you've seen that you've liked? Why?
7. Has your business marketed on-line? How is this done?

8. What challenges have you had developing the online part of your business?
9. What new business areas or industries have you considered marketing online?
10. What is your online business development strategy?

5. Leadership

1. Do you have any employees? Tell me about your employees?
2. What do you think motivates your employees these days?
3. What business speakers have you heard lately? What key learning did you take from their presentation?
4. What seminars or conferences have you sent your employees to that you'd recommend?
5. What are some of the key leadership trends in your industry today?
6. How does your company address these trends?
7. Do you have a structured training process for your employees?
8. What training have you found valuable? Technical? Leadership? Other?
9. What's the most effective management technique you've used?
10. In your view, what is the most important talent or skill that a leader must have?

Remember your goal is to get the other person talking about themselves as much as possible. As they answer the questions, be there, focus on them 100%, look at their face and nod your head, smile, whatever is appropriate for what is being said.

Business Referrals

One of the major reasons people attend business events is to meet other business people and hopefully do business together. Once people know, like and trust you (more on this concept later) they may be willing to do business with you. Moving down the path toward doing business by referral brings a totally different set of questions that can be asked.

I've deliberately kept this set of questions separate from the first fifty, as I believe you must not jump the gun here and try too hard too soon. Once you have spent quality time breaking the ice and getting to know the other person it may be appropriate to ask whether they may be interested in doing business with you, or someone you know.

If I'm attending a business function with the view to finding new business opportunities, I have a very clear agenda in mind, so when I'm talking to a person for the first time I am evaluating them very carefully. Too many people attend business functions with no clear purpose or intention. If I attend a function, it is always for a specific reason or purpose. Typically, that might mean I am attending because I know a certain person is there who I want to meet and connect with them.

Alternately, if there is no one person I want to meet, I usually set myself a goal for a certain number of new people I want to meet and have a meaningful conversation with. The number will depend on the type of function I'm attending and whether there is a longer period for meeting others. Usually my number is three new people. I want to meet three new people and find out enough about them to decide whether there may be a business connection that I can pursue.

While I'm engaging with new people, I'm evaluating them based on the following criterion. Can I do business with this person or would they have a need for my product or service? If the answer is no, the next criterion is: Can someone in my Key 4 do business with them? My Key 4 are my closest business friends, the people who support me in my business and are complimentary to what I do. If the answer is still no. Can they connect me with someone I would like to meet? If the answer is still no, I have two options at this stage:

1. Tactfully stop talking to them and move on to find someone else to meet with and connect.
2. Enjoy the conversation and know that no business will come from this conversation. By the way, it's OK to just enjoy a conversation, however remember your primary purpose is to talk to people to find business opportunities!

Now when you attend a function you can go with a focused mindset, be focused on the other person and also be focused on a mutually beneficial outcome i.e. doing business together. Once you have broken the ice and think that the other person may be suitable or interested in doing business with you, go ahead and ask one or more of the following questions.

Business Referral Clever Questions

1. What are your preferred ways to develop new business opportunities?
2. Who can I connect you with, who would be beneficial for your business?
3. How do you manage strategic alliances in your field?
4. Have you explored creating strategic alliances? (If yes. What were the results?)
5. What are some ways we might be able to work together?
6. What would you like more of in your business? What would you like less of?
7. What are some challenges you've experienced in this past year?
8. Who would be an ideal referral for your business?
9. What should I be listening for when I speak to others that would indicate a good referral for you?
10. If I could introduce you to the perfect person to do business, who would that be? What is their name?

Relationship Building Action Steps

1. Go prepared to any function with some Clever Questions.

2. Develop 5-10 of your favourite clever questions that you can use almost anywhere.

3. Practice using these questions, so they roll off your tongue easily.

4. Aim to get the other person talking as much as possible.

5. Use even more clever questions to move the conversation forward.

Chapter 8

But Wait, There's Even More Questions!
'EST' Questions

Once you get better and more experienced at asking questions you will develop your favourite few that work every time for you and you will become more fluent at asking questions. Once you become fluent you will be more adventurous and can begin to ask what I call 'EST' questions.

'EST 'questions are words that end in EST and usually require some more detailed explanation by the other person.

It could run like this...What do you do? Here's ten simple examples:

1. I'm a taxi driver. What's the biggest trip you've ever taken with a passenger?
2. I'm an airline pilot. What's the longest flight you've ever taken?
3. I'm an accountant. What's the biggest tax refund you've ever seen?
4. I'm a sign writer. What's the largest sign you've ever done?
5. I'm a cleaner. What's the messiest clean up job you've ever done?

6. I'm a teacher. Tell me about the sharpest student you ever taught.
7. I'm a personal trainer. Tell me about the scrawniest client you've ever worked with.
8. I'm a personal stylist. Oh, tell me about the vainest person you've ever worked with.
9. I'm a professional speaker. I believe it harder to make a shorter speech than a longer one, tell me about the briefest speech you've ever made.
10. I'm a surveyor. Tell me about the remotest place you've ever worked.

EST Words

Here's a list of fifty EST words to get you thinking. Trust me there are many, many more EST words in the English language and all can be used to ask insightful questions in a conversation.

50 EST Words

Biggest	Dishonest	Kindest	Queerest	Tardiest
Busiest	Earthiest	Longest	Remotest	Tenderest
Angriest	Easiest	Loudest	Richest	Tiniest
Boldest	Fairest	Meanest	Runniest	Unhappiest
Briefest	Flashiest	Messiest	Saddest	Unluckiest
Calmest	Gloomiest	Naughtiest	Scrawniest	Vainest
Cheekiest	Greatest	Newest	Sharpest	Wackiest
Commonest	Hardest	Plumpest	Sweetest	Weakest
Deadliest	Happiest	Prettiest	Swampiest	Youngest
Dearest	Jolliest	Quaintest	Tackiest	Zestiest

These questions will surely get the other person talking as they recall a specific example and allow you to ask more open-ended questions.

Another nice way to open the conversation and get someone else to tell you more about them is to simply say, "WOW! I would really like to know more about that".

Closed Questions

The problem with closed questions is that they normally shut down conversations and lead to yes or no answers. If you are seeking to get someone talking, then avoid closed questions. On the other hand, a closed question can come in handy at times, if you must close off a conversation and move on to talk with someone else. They too have a time and place in conversations.

A simple way to divert a conversation or close it off could be to say something like "Well that's interesting, my coffee cup is empty, would anyone like a top up?" The likely response is either yes or no. This will effectively break the pattern and most likely close off that conversation as you leave to top up your coffee.

Here are some other examples of closed questions:

Is the speaker starting after dinner is served?
Oh, you're a public accountant, do you have to work long hours?
What time do we finish?
How many staff do you have?
Do you work overseas?

Depending on the skill of the person being asked the question will depend on how these questions are answered. They could turn them into open-ended questions, or they could simply deliver a finite answer.

If we examine the first question one answer could simply be yes. An alternate answer could explain the order of proceedings, some comments about the food service and the talent or qualities of the speaker. Again, it depends on the skill of the person answering the question. It's better to ask a clever question, which forces a longer dialogue. These questions could be answered in a similar manner.

It really is better to know the right questions than to have all the answers!

Relationship Building Action Steps

1. Prepare a few EST Questions that you can use in varying situations.

2. Practice using your EST Questions, so that they roll off your tongue easily.

3. Avoid asking Closed questions as they shut down conversations.

Chapter 9

Find the Common Ground

The Plumber

I found the plumber through my cousin's husband. I didn't know any plumbers; however, my cousin Beverley was married to a carpenter, Phillip Ragonesi. My cousin was really like my sister. Let me explain, I'm the youngest of five boys, no sisters in my family. My Dad and his brother lived side by side, so my cousin Beverley was my sister, she just lived next door. Bev is six months younger than me, so we were very close. In my network, she's a Great and a Go To.

Her husband Phillip is a top bloke and being a carpenter was a Guru, a Great and a Go To for me and my building project. In activating my network, I spoke to Phillip very early in the piece and told him about the holes in my list. One of the holes was a plumber.

At the time, Phillip played rugby league football and one of the guys he played with was a plumber. They often referred business to each other and both knew of the others work on the football field and in the building field. The thing is, what brought them together was the common ground of football. They may never have met but for their love of sport.

The plumber's name was Tony. As soon as Tony arrived on site I knew we were going to get along. No, it wasn't my love of football or sport, in fact anyone who knows me, understands I couldn't care less about sport. As soon as Tony arrived on site he got out his radio. All building sites have one, two or sometimes even more radios going to keep the 'tradies' (An Australian slang term for a tradesperson) company as they work. The problem is sometimes they are all tuned to different stations. A cacophony of sound follows.

I had my radio going when he arrived and he proceeded to get out his radio and set it up at the other end of the house. When he turned it on, it was loud and tuned to a different station. Moments later I noticed something interesting happened. Tony retuned his radio to match my station, he then called out, "Can't have two stations running in opposition of each other, can we?". What a great gesture and a nice way to create some common ground between us. Tony understood one of the basics of getting into relationship, find some common ground.

If you find something that you have in common with the other person it makes it a whole lot easier to build a relationship with them. Tony's other great love was the Broncos rugby league football team. On the weekends, he worked as a Strapper for the A Grade team, a strapper runs on the field during play, giving the players a drink of water, sometimes strapping their injured arms or legs with tape and often providing instructions covertly from their coach. He did try to engage me with a conversation about football, however he quickly learned he was talking to the wrong person.

He was smart enough to steer away from football onto other topics that we were both interested in. Today Tony has now hung up his tool belt and works full time for his beloved Broncos supporting the A Grade team by running onto the field to supply water, wise words or whatever.

What's the Process?

The next step in the process of building relationships quickly is to find the common ground between you and the other person. This is an interesting step in the process and again has several components to it. Nearly everyone I have met has something in common with me.

Typically, at this stage I am going to look or listen for something we have in common. An easy one to look for is a wedding or engagement ring, it just so happens that I am married with two adult children. If I notice a ring, which may indicate that they are married, (there's no guarantee after all). I might ask, "Are you married, do you have kids?" In today's world people may be married, separated and with or without kids and still wear a wedding ring. Some people may have kids and not be married of course.

I figure the more generic the question at this moment the safer it is. They can answer and reveal as much as they want depending on the health of their relationship. If I sense the relationship is not healthy, I will move onto a different area of common ground.

Let's say, they answer, "Yes, I'm married and yes I have kids too". My next question is going to be aimed at finding more common ground, you see I have a daughter and a son, so I can talk easily about both sexes, about the joys, trials and tribulations of girls and boys. Not only that my kids are adults, so I can cover babyhood, the teenage years and leaving home, getting engaged and the challenges of each stage.

Other people would describe this as small talk and dismiss it as an inconsequential phase in a business relationship. I believe this is the spark where real relationships begin.

A Simple One

Start by finding a simple area of common ground and build on it as time passes. At a business function, you may not have a lot of time to explore common ground, however I believe this is the moment to establish something in common, so you can build rapport quickly to move to the next stage.

There are some simple common ground topics to start and as always there are some things to avoid, so let's examine a few of these and give you some pointers.

Sport

Often a safe topic to start is sport, most people have a passion for some kind of sport. Football is a big topic in Australia and depending on the State you live in will dictate the football code you follow. The easy part about sport is finding whether the other person has an interest or not, the tricky part can be if they support a different team to you.

It's at this moment that you have to remember the end goal here, getting into a relationship, not offending the other person with your one-eyed views on the supremacy of your team. There's a fine line here and I've been in conversations where it started out as friendly banter about opposing teams and ended in terse words and a clear disassociation between two people over their team's prowess in the competition.

I'm not much of a sports fan, so I have benign views about football, cricket or whatever. This works against me sometimes as I have trouble holding a conversation with someone with whom I want to deepen a relationship. I gently try to steer the conversation to another topic. Depending on the situation, I may even shut down the conversation and say something like "I'm the youngest of five boys, all my brothers love their sport, unfortunately I'm the black sheep of the family, it just doesn't interest me".

I'm only going to do this if I've found other significant areas of common ground or perhaps I've decided that this person is not someone I wish to develop a deeper relationship with.

One of my friends sold industrial water filters, I remember him avidly reading the sports pages one Sunday morning over brunch boning up on the cricket results as he had an appointment later that day with a client who loved cricket. He said to me, "I want to do business with this guy and he loves his cricket, if I'm going to hold a conversation with him, I need to be able to sound at least somewhat knowledgeable about his passion."

The client had chosen the common ground and that was a weak spot for him, however he knew the importance of having a common interest, so he brushed up, often just before they met.

Religion, Sex, Politics

I've grouped religion, sex and politics together as they are three topics I steer away from in general conversation. I respect people may have different religious views to mine and they have every right to them, I don't believe a business setting is the place to discuss religion at any time.

Sadly, there is a lot of conflict in the world based around religious beliefs. I think it would be nicer if all religions could practice more tolerance and respect for each other's views.

Sex again is not a topic for discussion at any time for me. People's preferences or habits in this arena are entirely their business. It's just too personal a topic to discuss in public.

Finally, politics, a truly dangerous minefield. I learnt an interesting lesson about building relationships and politics when I was just 19 years old. I worked at a customs agency in the City and at lunch time we would go to the lunch room for exactly one hour and eat our lunch, talk about stuff, tell jokes, you get the idea.

One day the topic of politics came up. In Australia, there are pretty much two major political parties, there are many other smaller ones. However, on this day I engaged in a "discussion" with another young man at my office, he too was just 19 years old. It went like this; he supported and voted for one party and I supported and voted for the other party. I can't even remember the catalyst for this conversation however, the outcome was that our conversation escalated into a shouting match with him vigorously supporting his party and me mine.

At 1p.m. our official lunch hour was over so with a scowl and filthy looks, we agreed to disagree and walked back to our desks in an uncomfortable silence. When I reached my desk, the wise old owl that sat behind me tapped me on the shoulder. "Come with me young fella". He walked me outside the building and said something like "Whilst I agree with your views on politics you have to realise that shouting at someone else just because they hold a different view to yours is not going to make them change their mind".

I learnt an extremely important lesson that day about relationships. In order to get into a relationship, if you have an opposing view it's sometimes better to keep your mouth shut.

To this day, I will not get involved in a political discussion, although I have been standing in a group where politics was discussed. I will leave this one up to you; as to whether you get involved or not. Remember relationships are not made or broken based on just one common ground topic, I just prefer to stay well away from this one.

Other Topics

The list is endless in terms of what to talk about to find the common ground. I have met people on the other side of the world and discovered we were both Boy Scouts and loved camping. I once met a guy in a hotel club lounge in Kuala Lumpur, Malaysia. The lounge offered cocktails and snacks at 5p.m. and the lounge was on the top floor with a magnificent view toward the famous Petronas Twin Towers.

I was travelling on business and was alone, this guy was also sitting alone and we were both staring at the magnificent view for some time sipping our drinks. Always the relationship builder, I struck up a conversation with him. He told me he used to live in East Germany before the Berlin Wall came down, he described his life both before and after. It sure was an interesting story.

He now worked for a company in a sales role and was in town meeting suppliers and prospects for his region. In his current role, he travelled extensively and visited Asia often. A picture of our common ground was forming, I travel extensively with my work, and I visit Asia regularly for work.

He kept staring at the view and eventually said, "You know what I really love? I've come to realise, it's my freedom". Man did that strike a chord with me! He nailed it, freedom. You see I worked in the Federal Government in Australia for a total of twenty-three years, working in the Australian Taxation Office, the Queensland Health Department; our main Government Health Department and the Brisbane City Council, our main local governing body. I had successfully negotiated my way through three tiers of Government, Commonwealth, State and Local.

I was literally sick of working with "turkeys" as I called them, starting my own business was a breath of fresh air and my freedom from bureaucracy.

Something happened from that moment forward, our conversation flowed, we had found the common ground, which was very significant for both of us.

Take a moment to consider what the common ground could be between you and the other person. If you get stuck here's a few ideas you could throw into the conversation:

- The suburb where you live
- Favourite holiday destination
- Favourite TV-show
- The car you drive
- Where you bought your shoes
- The pen you use
- The networking functions you like to attend
- Your hobby
- Youri sport
- Favourite sporting team
- The phone you own (iPhone, Android)
- The computer you use (Mac, PC)
- Your kid's hobbies
- Your kid's sport
- Your kid's school
- The school you went to
- Clubs you belong to
- Favourite recording artist
- Music genere
- The airline you prefer
- Your favourite clothing store
- Favourite shopping centre
- Favourite business author
- Business hero
- Last business book you read

That should keep you going for a while, of course the list is endless. These are simply suggestions, somewhere to start.

Enthusiasm Can Be Contagious

One secret ingredient I must mention here is enthusiasm. You must show some enthusiasm when you are discussing your common ground topic. If you are seriously into this common ground topic, then show the other person you are enthusiastic. If you aren't then you better be good at faking or just let it drop. You must be congruent of course and I've often seen boring people spark up once I touch the common ground nerve. It's like someone flicked the power switch and they came alive.

I think one of the hardest places to establish common ground is at a function with your significant other, your husband, wife, boyfriend or girlfriend. It's their safe ground and you are kind of left out like a shag on a rock, because it's not your territory. In our early married days, my wife was a breast-feeding counsellor with a community group called, Nursing Mothers Association of Australia. This organisation, now known as Breastfeeding Australia and does amazing work teaching new mothers how to breast-feed their children, supporting them with information, education and ongoing support.

The organisation is run by volunteers and has local groups of mothers that meet and discuss mothering topics, plus bringing their kids to socialize together. These local groups are again led by volunteers who organize the meetings, provide the structure and offer their homes in which the meetings are held.

Before our first child, our daughter was born my wife joined the local group and received tremendous support and advice about the scary journey we were about to embark upon. Eventually my wife studied and qualified as a breast-feeding counsellor and became the local group leader and made herself available for the 24-hour counselling hotline to support other mothers, just as we had been.

As you can see we, well my wife was heavily involved! Now we often attended Nursing Mothers' functions where I was the official Plus One! Initially I didn't know a soul and whilst the conversation flowed easily between the ladies' present, it was not so easy for me, I was the outsider.

My counter to this was to be enthusiastic, particularly when I was introduced to another Plus One, or should I say another Nursing Mother's father. I guess you could say the initial common ground we had was being married to a Nursing Mother's member. I was always enthusiastic to meet other partners and explore what we had in common and find a way to move off the heady topics of why little Johnny wasn't feeding so well of late.

Enthusiasm isn't easy to manufacture, though I've learned that if you can inject some enthusiasm whilst exploring common ground, it sure goes a long way toward making the conversation easier. Enthusiasm is contagious and I recommend you engage your enthusiasm drive in conversations and in the following circumstances

When you wake up in the morning.

When you wake up in the morning you have two choices, you can choose to make the day a great day or a disaster. Which do you choose? Open your eyes and make a conscious choice to enthusiastically greet the day, begin with a smile and a clear positive purpose. Enthusiasm is contagious and before long your family will be smiling and enthusiastic with you.

To encourage and inspire your co-workers, boss, key stakeholders.

When you get to work, share your enthusiasm with your co-workers, inspire them to make the day a great day. Focus on the common outcome you and your team will achieve for the day.

When meeting with clients, customers or prospects.

Share your enthusiasm with your prospects and clients, it is infectious and you will sweep them away with your enthusiasm. They will happily engage, ask more questions and may even buy more products.

When interacting with others online, In LinkedIn, Facebook, Twitter.

How many people do you know that post negative or downright depressing stuff on social media? Focus on being the positive enthusiastic person, you will soon notice the difference in the mood of your followers and your posts will be forwarded and followed by more enthusiastic people.

Enthusiasm can't be overrated, this is absolutely one of the best Secret Weapons when it comes to building relationships.

Make Them Curious

Building curiosity around what you do is another process that you can use in the common ground phase. Curiosity often results in questions and questions mean you are deepening your relationship with the other person. How do you create curiosity, I hear you ask?

You could take an opposing position or stand on an issue. This will surely lead to more conversation and debate. Be careful though, you don't want to go so far into opposition, that you create a disconnect.

Perhaps keep them guessing by withholding some information and build curiosity as you reveal the full details.

Relationship Building Action Steps

1. Listen carefully to identify what you may have in common with the other person and talk about that.

2. Avoid talking about contentious issues, which may include religion, sex, politics.

3. Remember enthusiasm is contagious, so be enthusiastic when talking about what you have in common.

4. Create some curiosity around what you are talking about, curiosity draws people in to want to know more and engage more.

Chapter 10

The P.S. Positive Service

Mark the Bolt Man

When you owner build a house in Australia, you must display a sign that says you are an owner builder and you must also display your permit number. Not long after I put up my sign the sales 'reps' started to drop in to introduce themselves. Some were better at relationship building than others. One day a guy dropped by, his name was Mark. I can't remember his last name as I just knew him as Mark, Mark the Bolt Man. You see, Mark worked for a company called Action Fasteners. He sold nails, screws, bolts, basically any fasteners a builder would need.

Mark was good at relationships, he was carpenter by trade, though had decided to hang up his tools and become a sales 'rep'. He spent the day visiting building sites and selling his wares. When he arrived, he did his best to establish the common ground as quickly as possible. He just lived up the street and around the corner. He had recently moved in after owner building his house as well. Straight away we had a lot in common.

Mark was clever, he knew his building codes and he knew relationships. He established the common ground and then he took it to the next level, he offered to help out. He created a positive service experience, a way to help me above and beyond what others were offering.

After a lot of conversation about my plan, my progress and where-to-next, he offered to become my official supplier of fasteners for the project. The deal was, he would drop in on his way home from work, have a chat, take my order and drop off the supplies on his way home the next day. This worked a treat. Some days he went home with my shopping list written on a piece of 90 x 45mm pine wall stud. The problem was paper was often in short supply on the building site and timber was plentiful! Being the resourceful type that I am, I made good use of the prolific supply of timber on site.

Mark set himself apart from the crowd by finding a way to serve me and make my job easier.

Think about this concept for a moment, how could you serve others to enhance the relationship that you have?

P.S. Positive Service

I mentioned earlier that my brother Neville was a great keeper-in-toucher, yes, a technical term! In the early days, he did this by letter, he lived in Darwin in the Northern Territory for a period of about eleven years through the seventies and early eighties. Every week he would write a letter to my mother and every week my mother would write a letter to Neville. On Sunday night, Mum would always be sitting at the kitchen table writing to Neville filling him in on what we had been up to in the week just past.

Often a letter would be written and signed off with Mum's standard farewell, "That's all the news for this week, love Mum." Of course, the word "mum" was signed with a flourish! Then course another thought popped into her head and she would add a Post Script or what we know as a P.S.

The initials P.S. stand for post script and comes from the Latin term, post scriptum, meaning written after. The P.S. is used by letter writers all around the world and is often an after-thought or idea, which cannot be left out and relates to the original text and always adds value to the communication. You could say a P.S. is a vital part of the communication.

I want to take this idea and relate it to relationships, the P.S. Or Positive Service is a vital part of establishing and maintaining a relationship. The P.S. may seem like an after-thought;however, the clever relationship builder knows that the P.S. is the key to cementing a long-lasting relationship. Serving others is the key to great relationships. I apply the P.S. to as many situations as I can to enhance my relationships.

Serving Others

Let's step off the building site now and head out to a networking function. How can you serve others in a function room? There are hundreds of ways.

I was at a conference in the USA recently, it's lunchtime and I'm standing in the buffet queue waiting for my food. I finally reach the table and grabbed a plate. Instead of filling it with food, I turned to the guy behind me, read his name badge and said, "Hi Kevin, here's a plate for your lunch". Kevin and I had never met before; however, he was taken aback by my gesture and pleasantly surprised. We began chatting as we filled our plates, we then sat together and continued chatting over lunch.

We shared lots of information with each other, found out we both have a love for camping, we both enjoy a glass of red wine and we are both professional speakers. Kevin and I have become second best friends for life! Okay, I may be exaggerating just slightly, however, I have an open invitation to visit Kevin at his home in Kentucky and stay in his house as his guest. We are still keeping in touch by email and looking forward to catching up again at next year's conference in the USA.

All this from a small act of positive service, I simply took the time to call the guy by his name and hand him a plate for his lunch.

That's an easy one, so what else can you do? Here's a list of possible small acts of Positive Service:

1. Offer to get a cup of coffee or tea for someone.
2. Hold a seat for someone at a busy function.
3. Open a door and hold it open as they pass through.
4. Offer to take a photo of a group of people, when you see them struggling to do the obligatory selfie.
5. Offer to send someone an article that relates to what you have just been talking about.
6. Offer to introduce someone to a particular person they want to meet in the room.
7. Offer to sample their product in return for a positive testimonial.
8. Pay for someone else's coffee/tea.
9. Send someone you have worked with an unsolicited testimonial on LinkedIn.
10. Refer someone a piece of business or recommend them to another interested business colleague.

These are just ten examples of hundreds and possibly thousands of ways to serve other people. The key here is to just do something simple, yet meaningful for the other person. Note the examples I've given of Positive Service are small, yet simple. You could go all out and spend heaps of money, you could buy expensive restaurant meals, tickets to sporting matches and even send a gift of your product to the other person. I think you have to be careful and be seen as someone that genuinely cares. Remember this Positive Service is simply a way to get into a relationship, it is not a way to bribe your way into a business deal.

The overwhelming response or reaction you want from this Positive Service, is to have the other person notice you and feel good about you or the experience. This should then cement your relationship a little further and can then lever off that into a deeper relationship.

Compliments

Using compliments is another way that you can serve someone. I'm a great believer in giving positive compliments that will give the other person a boost, making them feel good about the interaction they are having with you and ultimately leaving them with a good impression of you as a person. Be careful here, I don't mean giving compliments which will ultimately lead to an obvious benefit for you.

Let me give you an example. I've been shopping with my wife many times over the years. We go into a clothes' shop and typically the staff will greet you, say hello, perhaps offer to assist you by asking if you are looking for something in particular. When it comes time to try a garment on, a dress, some slacks or whatever, the comments from the sales assistant can be excessively positive. "Oh, that looks perfect on you!""Oh, that colour is just you!""Oh, that's gorgeous, let me get the matching shoes and belt for you to try on."

Can you see where I'm going here? They have no real interest in my wife or how she looks, they simply want a sale. I have literally seen women come out of a change room in poorly fitted clothes that obviously don't suit their body shape and the sales assistant is raving about the colour or whatever, simply because they want the customer to feel good and then buy something.

If you are going to make a compliment, make it genuine. I have a BS radar that detects fake comments from a country mile away and I suspect a lot of people do also.

If you are going to compliment someone choose something that they have had a part in creating. My mother loved brown eyes and often commented about children and their brown eyes, the problem with this is that you have no choice whether you have brown eyes or not. I'm not trying to beat up my mother here, I simply want to make the point to compliment wisely.

I suggest that you pay people a compliment about something in which they have had to make a choice. I love shoes and those who know me would recognise that I often wear a different pair every day. I have been accused of being a male Imelda Marcos. In case you don't know, Imelda Marcos was the wife of Ferdinand Marcos, the former President the Philippines from 1965 to 1986 and largely remembered for his brutal rule of the country. Imelda on the other hand was remembered for her excessive shoe collection. On fleeing the country after their martial law collapsed in 1986 protestors stormed the Malacanang Palace to discover Imelda had left behind 2,700 pairs of shoes in her wardrobe. Note, that's what she left behind!

Now I sure don't have that many pairs, however I have an appreciation for shoes and I look at what other people wear and if I see a unique pair or something that catches my eye, I will always make a positive compliment. This serves two purposes, to make the compliment an act of Positive Service and to establish more common ground with the other person.

Another thing I look out for is jewellery worn by women in particular. Sweeping generalization here, most women love to wear nice jewellery, not all, most. If I see a nice ring or bracelet I will always compliment the woman. It's amazing the stories that have emerged as a result of paying a compliment about a piece of jewellery. Many times, it is a treasured family heirloom, or perhaps was bought for them by a loved one for a special occasion. Generally, women in Australasia wear their wedding and engagement rings on the left hand, in Europe they often wear them on the right hand. Either way, depending on which country I'm in, if I notice a nice engagement ring and wedding band, I will make a positive comment.

One of my favourite lines is "Wow! Look at those rings, someone likes you!" Of course, I'm paying a compliment and I'm honouring the fact that they are in a relationship with someone special. The reaction is usually a gushing thank you and a story about the lady's husband and what a lovely guy he is. I've never had this one back fire on me yet. It's a favourite of mine while I'm checking in for my seat on an airplane. Because I fly a lot, I've learned that if you can get into a relationship quickly with the staff member checking you in. My Positive Service in the form of a compliment sometimes results in them returning the favour and upgrading me. Like everything in life, there's no guarantee about this working, however, it is nice just to see the glow my comments create.

The Law of Reciprocity

In his best-selling book, "Influence, the Psychology of Persuasion," author Robert Cialdini writes about the six universal principles of influence. One of these universal principles is what social psychologists call the "Law of Reciprocity," if I help you, you will help me in return. Cialdini researched this topic over thirty-five years and gives amazing examples of how this reciprocity just kicks in automatically. If you do something for someone, the theory is they will return the favour to you.

First published in 1984 and still as relevant today as it was then, this concept needs to be carefully considered in the relationship building process. If you perform a Positive Service for another person they will look to find a way to return your small act of service. If I buy you coffee, next time we meet, it's very likely you will return the favour and pay for the coffee.

Unscrupulous types have used this principle to manipulate people into buying decisions that they may not normally consider. Many years ago, my parents-in-law were holidaying on the Gold Coast with their son to celebrate his graduation from high school. It was years ago, as today the graduating kids go to the beach on their own to participate in a ritual called 'Schoolies Week', without their parents and usually with copious amounts of energy, fuelled by alcohol and maybe even drugs. Whoops! that's another story.

Back to my parents-in-law. They were walking along doing some window shopping at Surfers Paradise, a famous Australian tourist destination. It was about midday anda nice young woman steps out of a doorway and says, "Are you on holiday?" Of course, they reply yes and before you know it they are eating a "free lunch" at a new resort nearby and by about two o'clock that afternoon had bought a stake in a brand new time share resort at Surfers Paradise. They were not in the market for a stake in a time share resort and when I asked them why they bought, the answer started with, "Well we had this nice lunch and..."

They were victims of the Law of Reciprocity used inappropriately.

Why am I telling you this? I am a great believer in the positive outcomes of the Law of Reciprocity. I believe that if you genuinely help someone, then the Law of Reciprocity will kick in and you will receive something good in return. Notice I didn't say you will receive something in return from the person you helped. I know from years of giving that if you give, you will receive, however sometimes your rewards come from another place. It's a universal principle and hard for some people to grasp.

If you go to my LinkedIn profile, you can read many testimonials about the work I've done over the last 17 years I've been in business. I started out on LinkedIn not really knowing or understanding what I was doing. At night, I would sit at my kitchen table and send connection messages to people that went something like this. "I see that we have several mutual connections, thought that we should connect directly".

This simple script saw my LinkedIn community grow past 500, then 5,000 and today I'm well over 11,000 connections. I'm in the top 10% of viewed profiles and I get a lot of business from LinkedIn. Here's where it gets interesting though. On LinkedIn, you can recommend other people and you can ask for a recommendation. I never ask for a recommendation; however, I regularly recommend other people. The responses I get for genuinely complimenting people about their expertise or a service they have provided is delightful. Next of course, they want to return the favour and within a day or two of recommending others, guess what? I get a recommendation.

Now for the really interesting part, sometimes the recommendation comes from the person I just recommended and other times it comes out of the blue from someone else. It's the positive Law of Reciprocity in action. A 'P.S.' positive service compliment goes a long way.

Relationship Building Action Steps

1. Think of ways you can deliver a P.S. to someone in your network every day.

2. Develop a list of your favourite ways to serve others. Then implement them regularly.

3. Make an effort to genuinely compliment someone every day.

4. Remember the Law of Reciprocity, what goes around, comes around. Be positive in your every thought, word and action and positivity will return to you.

5. Write a positive recommendation for someone on LinkedIn based on your experience of them every day. Stand back and wait for the avalanche of recommendations to flow back to you.

Chapter 11

Can I Do Business With This Person?

The Printer from Networking Hell

I'm a great believer in the power of the Chamber of Commerce. I belong to my local Chamber and have spoken many times at various Chambers of Commerce around Australia sharing my business message. It's a great environment to meet and hang out with other local small business people. You get to know each other, build some trust and perhaps do some business with each other. It's also just a great place to share ideas and learn something new from the guest speakers or the members themselves. It's a good place to be on so many levels.

Except for when you meet the "Printer from Networking Hell". I went along to the monthly Chamber meeting a few months back and being the Relationships Guy I always make a point of speaking to someone I don't know. Perhaps they are a guest or a new member. I try to make them welcome and help them understand what a friendly bunch of people we are and that there's always someone they can talk with at the meeting. I guess I'm walking the Relationship Guy talk!

At this meeting, a few months back a new guy appears. I start at step one of the ten step Relationships Guy Model and shake hands and introduce myself. Now this guy is no slouch at networking. No sooner had I introduced myself than he's right on the front foot asking what I do. I gave him a short answer, something like "I'm known as the Relationships Guy, I speak at conferences and seminars and run training workshops teaching business owners and sales people how to get into a relationship quickly". Before I could respond with and what do you do? He launched.

It was a full-on sales pitch. "Well, Lindsay, if you speak at conferences and run training seminars and workshops, you must produce workbooks for your participants?" I answered "Well, yes I do". Cutting me off, he jumped straight in; "I thought so and it's timely that we have met because I have a full-service printing company, I can deliver all of your printing needs. I print workbooks, in either black and white or full colour, I'm guessing you would really prefer full colour?"

I opened my mouth to respond, no need really, he wasn't interested in my response. "In fact, not only can I do workbooks, I can do your promotional flyers, I can do your fully branded notepads for your participants and I can even do individual name plates for your course participants. This month we are doing a special on business cards, I'm guessing that you must attend a lot of functions like this and probably like me, you give out a lot of cards. We can do them in full colour, double sided with cello glaze, I've done some really neat folding jobs and I have some real nice examples of embossed cards, which would absolutely make you stand out from the rest of the pack."

It was at this moment that I think he stopped for a micro second to draw breath. Can you guess what my response was? I said something like "Oh, that's amazing, welcome to the Chamber, I'm sorry I've just spotted someone I have to speak with, please excuse me". That may sound a little short, however it was no problem for our printer, he had already latched onto the next hapless bystander and was delivering his pitch at a blistering pace.

I don't know about you; however, I am never going to do business with anyone like this guy. He just didn't care about me as a person, there was no attempt to get to know me, find some common ground, all he wanted was an opportunity to sell me something.

Why do we Network?

One of the primary reasons we go to business functions is to meet people and to try and expand our networks. An outcome of expanding our network is the hope that we will meet other business people who may be interested in doing business with us firstly and then perhaps finding someone with whom you can do business, someone who has goods or services which you want or need.

Again, the primary reason we want to get into a relationship quickly with someone is to figure out if we can do business together. I've met some lovely people over time at networking functions only to realise that we are never going to do business together. They may be direct competitors or perhaps they don't share the same target market as me, so it's unlikely I will ever be able to refer them any business. However, they are still nice people and we are never going do business together.

Part of the process of relationship building in business is to figure out if you can do business with the person you are speaking to. Here's my process when I meet someone new. I will greet them enthusiastically and get them talking about themselves and their business. I will ask them questions to try to figure out if they fit my target market. At all times, I'm applying the ten-step relationship model. I want to focus on them 100%, find some common ground and perhaps find a way to serve them if appropriate.

Initially I am probably just going to focus on them and find our common ground and more importantly I am going to get them to do most of the talking. As I've mentioned before I'm applying the 80/20 rule here.

The 80/20 rule was made famous by Vilfredo Pareto, an Italian engineer, sociologist, economist and philosopher. He made several contributions to the world of economics and was the first to discover that income follows a Pareto distribution. The Pareto principle was named after him and is based on his observations that 80% of the land in Italy was owned by just 20% of the population. This distribution has been popularized across many disciplines since and is now universally referred to as the 80/20 rule.

Once I have them talking I begin to assess if they are a true prospect for me, are they part of my target market? Could they be a buyer of my services?

If I determine that they aren't a real prospect, I will now assess my options. I could stop talking to them right now or figure out whether they are a prospect for one of my referral circle buddies. I'll talk more about referral circles later, for the moment they are close business associates who share my target market and do not compete with me. If they fit the target market and could be a prospect for one of my referral circle buddies, I will keep talking and try to get enough information from them so that I can refer them.

Finally, if they aren't a prospect for me, or one of my referral circle buddies, I will stop talking to them. Of course, I'm going to do that in the nicest possible way, however the point is that if this person isn't a business prospect, it's best to spend your time talking with someone who is.

So, it comes down to just three options:

Yes

No

Maybe?

A Little Mercenary

I'm guessing a part of you is thinking, hang on isn't that all a little too mercenary? Is that what networking and business functions are all about? Just meeting people to figure out if I can do business with them or not and if not move on? It does really depend on why you have attended the function in the first place.

I believe that you must have a clear goal or intention about the whole event that you are attending. Ask yourself these questions before you leave home:

1. Am I going to meet and seek out new prospects?

2. Am I going to simply catch up with friends, associates and existing clients and re-engage with them so they remember me?

3. Am I going only to listen to the speaker and learn new information?

4. Am I going for all of the above reasons?

Once you decide what your intention is, I strongly recommend that you make a plan according to your goal or intention for that particular function. Let's address each of the four points individually.

1. Are you going to meet and seek out new prospects?

Great, if this is your intention, then you have to make a plan about exactly who or how many new prospects you are thinking of meeting. Set a goal for a specific number and don't stop talking and moving around the room until you have met your goal. I recommend that if you are seeking new prospects you set the number at no more than three.

You may actually have to speak to a lot more than three people before you find three prospects, remembering that you may meet and talk to a few "printers from networking hell" along the way. Keep talking and interacting until you have collected three business cards and have had meaningful conversations with three prospects.

A meaningful conversation is one where you have met, found some common ground and perhaps given a small act of service, you have discussed the possibility of assisting each other and made a tentative follow up meeting or floated the idea of catching up in the near future. Once you have achieved this, move on to the next conversation.

An alternate strategy is to go with the primary intention of meeting a specific person, with a view to getting them interested in what you do enough, so that they are willing to have a follow-up meeting with you in the near future to discuss how you may be able to assist each other.

If you are going to meet a specific person, I suggest you also think about who you know who already knows that person. Would they be willing to introduce you and promote you in the best light to the person you wish to meet? I have used this strategy many times with great effect. In fact, I rarely go to a business function without a wingman or a buddy that will work with me. More about the Wingman Strategy.

The Wingman Strategy

As I said earlier, I never go to a business function alone, I always take along a wingman or wing buddy, someone I trust who knows me well and is willing and able to promote me, just as I am willing and able to promote them.

Here's how it works. Before the business function we meet and discuss our strategy, we talk about who we want to meet and what we will say about each other to get the target person interested in meeting with either me or them at a later date.

Let me recount a real story. I spoke at my Chamber of Commerce meeting and offered for the members to come along to a two-hour introductory session on "How to do Business by Relationship". Two branch managers from a major bank, Jill and Sharon came along to my session and loved the principles and concepts I shared at the session. One of these managers says to me, "You must meet our boss, the Regional Manager, your material is perfect for our business".

By chance we were all going to be attending a function just ten days later. At the function, my wing buddy Sharon, the Branch Manager steers me over to her boss, Wayne, the Regional Manager and introduces me. It went something like this...

"Wayne, let me introduce you to Lindsay Adams, the Relationships Guy." We did the usual stuff, shook hands and made some small talk. Then my wing buddy launched her attack. "Wayne, let me tell you more about what Lindsay does. He is known as the Relationships Guy because that's exactly what he does best, he builds relationships quickly and he trains other people how to do it also. He's brilliant, in fact Jill and I from Stafford Branch went along to one of his sessions and it was amazing. We learned so much about how to get into relationship quickly and even better, how to leverage those relationships to meet more people and make more sales. His processes are so simple, yet powerful."

"In fact," she continued "What Lindsay teaches would be perfect for our regional team and is right in line with our service culture". She definitely had Wayne's interest here.

He says, "That sounds worthwhile, we should get together and meet, so I can learn more about what you do."

Note carefully how many words I have spoken up to this moment, absolutely none!

I open my mouth and say, "That would be great Wayne, how about we meet for lunch one day next week and I can go over what I do in detail." He agreed, we opened our diaries and set the date.

That whole process may have taken five minutes maybe.

The best part was I didn't even speak, my wing buddy did all the talking and effectively 'sold' me without me contributing more than a smile and a positive nod occasionally. Sharon was a great sales person for me and in fact she could say stuff that I couldn't. Imagine if the scene played out like this...

Me: "Wayne let me tell you about what I do, I'm the Relationships Guy, which is what I do best, I build relationships quickly and I teach other people to do it also. I'm brilliant! I even teach people how to leverage these relationships to meet more people and make more sales. What I teach is so simple, yet so powerful."

Wayne: Thinking to himself, "Well this guy is full of himself, he has an ego even I couldn't jump over, if he says much more, I'm going to vomit."

I just could not say the things about myself that Sharon did and this is exactly what you and your wing buddy are going to do when you go to a business function. You will talk about your wing buddy to their prospects and you will sing their praises. You can say all the good things that they can't get away with saying about themselves. Next, you will switch roles and your wing buddy will return the favour about you and your amazing skills.

The key here of course is the preparation, you must be prepared. You have to spend time with your wing buddy training them about your business and what you do. That is of course if they haven't already had a direct experience of what you do. Teach them the key words and phrases you want them to use to describe you. Take time to practice well before you attend your first event together. After you do it once or twice, it becomes second nature and easier and easier.

From this moment forward, never attend a business function alone again, always take a wing buddy with you. Go with a clear plan in mind for you and for your wing buddy, identify the person you want to meet and connect with, think about how many prospects you want to meet and keep talking and circulating until you've met your target. Then and only then can you both relax and catch up with your business friends in the room.

Oh, I'm happy to report that the lunch with Wayne turned into a $20,000 assignment and the beginning of a long-term business relationship. Woohoo!

2. Are you going to simply catch up with existing clients, friends and associates and re-engage with them so they remember you?

If your intention is simply to catch up with some existing clients, friends or associates then I still strongly recommend that you have a plan. You must still work with your wing buddy and think about how many clients you will touch base with before you go more free flow and just catch up with friends.

I never miss an opportunity to engage with previous clients and let them know what I'm up to. Think about it this way, perhaps they may be interested in re-hiring you for the new activity you are going to tell them about. Working with your wing buddy you can guide the conversation to highlight your current exciting product offering.

Let me give you a real-life example. I was at a function with Joanna, a wing buddy in Singapore. I work closely with Joanne, she is the Chief Operating Officer for STTS, a large training and consulting company.

She promotes me in Singapore and we attend functions together; she talks about me and I talk about the amazing range of services that her company offers.

We were at a large business function, had met our quota of prospects and were just catching up with friends and colleagues. Talking to one of Joanne's long-term clients and now a friend I managed to weave into the conversation that Joanne's company had just launched a senior leadership program, something that was totally new for them. The person we were speaking to, an old loyal client and had previously hired them for secretarial training, suddenly became very interested in this new offering.

This chance conversation led to a subsequent meeting and a nice piece of business for Joanne.

3. Are you going only to listen to the speaker and learn new information?

If you are going along just to listen to the speaker and learn new information, you still have to take along your wing buddy. Why? I hear you ask. Your wing buddy is one of your strongest allies and would most likely be a member of your Key 4, a concept we'll explore later. Suffice to say, this person will be heavily invested in your business and you in theirs. You will look for any and many opportunities to support each other, so take along your wing buddy so they can learn and grow from the experience as well.

Plus, you never know just who is going to be in the room, maybe, just maybe, there will be someone there worth meeting for you or for them.

4. Are you going for all of the above reasons?

If you are an all of the above person, then I think it's clear what you must do. Get clear on your goal or intention, train your wing buddy about who you want to meet and what to say to them. Once you have reached your goal, cruise the room, relax and re-connect with your clients, colleagues and friends. Always keep your eyes and ears open for an opportunity for you or your wing buddy.

Who is Your Ideal Wingman?

Here's the good news, you can have more than one wingman. The number you have depends on the number of functions you attend and the number of target markets you work in. I work extensively in the Venue Management Industry and attend networking functions for that industry in several states of Australia. When I attend a function in each different state, I have a different wingman. In some cases, this strategy works better than others due to the level of contact I have with the relevant wingman.

I also worked in the banking and finance industry, so when I attend functions for these industries, I need a different person to attend with me.

Here are some characteristics to look for in a potential wingman:

1. Someone you know, like and trust.
2. Someone who is willing to spend time learning about you and your business.
3. Someone who is coachable.
4. Someone who is willing to attend functions with you regularly.
5. Someone who listens well and is good at relationships.
6. Someone who is keen to grow their business and just as importantly, to grow yours.

Choosing a wingman should be a carefully thought through process. You want to make sure that this person understands the power of doing business by relationships and is willing to attend functions with you and work with you to further grow both your businesses.

Choosing and Training Your Wingman

I have sometimes stumbled on the perfect wingman at functions, just by engaging in relationship building conversations. If I see a synergy between our businesses and our personalities, I will simply invite them to coffee, with my standard invitation. "Hey Rob, it seems that you and I have a lot of synergy in business, I think we could help each other. What are you doing next Tuesday, have you got time for a coffee to explore some ideas I have that may benefit us both?"

Next step in the process is to meet and outline the wingman strategy and how it works. If they are interested or willing, then you must get serious and book additional time together to train them about your business. Just as important now, is that they train you about their business.

Here's some things to cover in the training:

The Benefits from Being Your Wingman

1. Help them understand the benefits to be gained by supporting each other.
2. Outline how the wingman strategy works and why it's better to have a wingman talk about you, than you talking about yourself.
3. Describe previous successful wingman relationships and the benefits gained.

Your Ideal Client

1. Give them a detailed description of the perfect client for you.
2. What they do.
3. Where they reside.
4. What they earn.
5. The typical industry they are engaged in.
6. Any prerequisites necessary before you can work with them.

7. Go over real-life examples of people you have worked with and the kind of work you have done for them.
8. What events they are likely to attend.

Your Product or Service Offering

1. List or show them the range of your products or services.
2. Tell them the pricing structure.
3. Tell them about your bulk purchase policy, your discounting or no discount policy.

Marketing Materials

- Walk them through the following marketing materials if you have them.
- Webpage
- Newsletters
- Flyers
- Brochures
- YouTube Channel
- Other videos

Definitions

- Help them understand any specific industry terms or slang words they may encounter.
- Define the various divisions or parts of the industry in which you specialize. In the venue industry, there are specific sectors, arenas, convention centres, stadiums, performing arts centres, exhibition halls, university centres and amphitheaters.
- Go over the names of all the products or services you offer and make sure they understand what they are, what they mean and what outcomes they deliver.

Showcase Pack

- Give them a sample pack of your best work. (A graphic designer wingman of mine gave me a presentation pack of his best designs showcasing each design category he worked.)
- Show them your best brochure or your website, so they can talk about it to others.

Your Networks

- Which networks do you belong to?
- What events do you attend?
- What are you known for in each network?
- What awards or recognitions have you earned at these networks?
- What hobbies do you have?

Action Plan

- What happens next?
- Agree a plan of action for further training perhaps.
- Agree to meet and practice what you would say about each other, role play is the best way to get this stuff in your head.
- Agree which functions you will attend together.
- Agree to meet or confer by phone before you arrive at the function to determine your plan for that function, who specifically do you want to meet, how many people you want to connect with?

Take baby steps at first, ease into this relationship and make sure you commit to learning just as much about their business as you teach them about yours. Remember this is a two-way street and the more you invest, the more you will get back in return.

Relationship Building Action Steps

1. Avoid the networking pounce. Networking is for relationship building, never selling.

2. When you are at a networking function, apply the 80/20 rule again. Spend 80% of your time talking to prospects, clients and new connections and 20% of your time with friends catching up.

3. When you go networking, have a clear goal or intention in mind before you go:

   a. Set the number of new connections you will make.

   b. Identify people you specifically want to meet and perhaps make an appointment to see later.

   c. Decide how much time you will spend re-engaging with clients and friends.

   d. Stick to your goals, once they are done, then relax.

4. Never network alone, always have a wingman with you.

5. Take time to identify and train a wingman before you start networking together.

6. It's OK to have more than one wingman, just use them one at a time.

Chapter 12

What Next? How To Initiate A Follow Up Meeting

By now you have been to a business networking function, you've met someone for the first time that you could probably do business or perhaps you've met someone with whom one of your referral circle could do business. What do you say next?

The worst possible thing you could say at this moment is something like "Wow, I reckon you are the perfect prospect for me, I can easily supply as many "widgets" (your product or service) as you can use each month, how many would you like to order?"

Even if you have the perfect prospect standing right in front of you and you know they need what you have, that moment is NOT the time to sell, unless of course they have invited you to tell them more, or they have asked you for a quote.

OK, so when is the time to sell? I hear you ask. The time to sell is right after you meet them for the first time. In a perfect world, you would find an opportunity to provide a P.S. Send them a gift, send them a copy of your book, send them the article you talked about, do something to cement the relationship further.

If you are talking to someone and they seem to be the perfect prospect for you, they have signaled they are interested in the products or services you offer or you simply "click" and you know that they could be a customer, move on to the next step. Depending on the situation I would say something like one of these statements:

1. "You know it seems like we have some interesting synergies, how about we meet for coffee next week to explore how we could help each other in business?"

2. "Wow, I think we could actually help each other in business, why don't we meet up next week for a coffee and explore some opportunities?"

3. "I think there is a definite fit between what I do and what you are looking to achieve, why don't we get together next week for a coffee and see how we can help each other?"

Note in every line, I want to meet them to see how we can help each other. I'm not meeting them to see how much of my products or services I can sell them, not overtly at least. It really is in the semantics. In reality, I do want to sell them something, however I have been in business long enough now to realise that it is often a two-way street. They may ultimately buy my product, which would actually help me a lot AND maybe it's a two-way street. They may have something I want to buy, maybe I can refer them on to someone else who wants their product or service. Keep an open mind here, remember to add a P.S.

I spoke at a networking function about doing business by relationship in Melbourne and one of the audience members spoke to me afterward and asked a lot of questions about the process I teach and how he could implement more relationship-based practices in his marketing firm. He was clearly a prospect for me and I could easily sell him further consulting services.

We got to a point where I said, "Rod, it seems like there's a good fit between what I do and some of the processes you have in place, though I think you could do some things a little better. I'm in Melbourne for two more days, why don't we get together tomorrow or the next day and see how we can help each other?" He responded, "Great can you come to my office at 10a.m. tomorrow".

The next day I went to his office and we talked more about what he was doing in terms of managing relationships in his business. I did what I call a Relationship Management Audit, where I focus on the relationship management practices in place and try to identify what's missing. I quickly identified a bunch of areas in which he could improve and made some suggestions about how he could do that. He was thrilled and agreed to engage me to improve their relationship management processes. Which was great!

What was even better was when he said, now enough about me, I have some referrals for you, suddenly he really had my attention! He went on to list three of his clients that he wanted me to talk to and he said that he had these people in mind to refer to me even before I suggested we get together. After our initial deep dive, using my Relationship Management Audit, he was certain that I could help these people.

The best part was he got straight on the phone to talk to them one by one and connected us straight away. I love opportunities like that.

If you are interested in a Relationship Management Audit you can drop me an email at lindsay@lindsayadams.com and I'll be happy to go through the process with you.

Relationship Building Action Steps

1. Practice how to set up a follow up meeting and make it clear that you are following up for a mutual benefit.

2. Consider having a Relationship management Audit done on your business. Drop me an email.

Chapter 13

Follow Up - Do What You Promised

The best part about leaving a good business event is having a couple of business cards in your pocket from people you have had a meaningful conversation with and you or your Key 4 could possibly do business together.

Leaving a networking event with a handful of great contacts is always a satisfying feeling. It means, to many of us, it has been a justifiable use of our valuable time and it helps us to feel that this investment in our business has not been a wasted opportunity. After all, our time spent networking has a value to it.

The key strategy is to follow up with the people you meet within 24 hours. It shows you to be on the ball and efficient as well as valuing the conversation you had. A good start for a new business relationship. If you receive a decent follow-up email, wouldn't it also be polite to reply? I am constantly amazed at how many people do not.

I visited a corporate trade show recently. It was put on a by a group of hotels to showcase their wares and to generate interest in their properties. What I found interesting was after the event. I visited twelve booths and had a conversation with representatives from each of the twelve hotels. We exchanged cards and some gave me additional information on the spot.

The next day, one person sent me an email saying how nice it was to meet me and if she could help in any way, to please contact her etc. etc. You know the sort of email it was, reasonably generic and probably the exact same text she sent out to everyone else she met that day. I replied saying it was nice to meet her and thanks for following up, promising to stay in touch should I need her services. A nice exchange.

Over the next four days guess how many other emails like this one I received...Exactly NONE!

Then suddenly one week to the day later, I received another generic email saying pretty much the exact same stuff and I responded in the same way. This time however, I received a more personal response from the sales rep.

I have to say, I'm surprised at the lack of follow up or acknowledgement of our contact at the show. If I exchange cards with someone, I generally email them, or send a hand-written note saying something about our meeting. In my mind it's just common courtesy, however in my business mind, it's another step towards a profitable relationship.

One of my long-term speaker friends, Robyn Henderson runs a business called Networking to Win www.networkingtowin.com.au. She is the most amazing person who follows up with people in such thoughtful ways. When it was her birthday a reminder came up on my phone. I hadn't spoken to Robyn in ages so decided on the spur of the moment to call and wish her a happy birthday and to catch up. We had a great old chat and filled each other in on what we had been up to in the intervening months since our last conversation.

During our conversation I mentioned two things, I was going to run in the Gold Coast Marathon and that the day after the marathon I was flying to America to attend the National Speakers Association Convention. I did both of those things and when I got home from the USA about three weeks after we had spoken, there was a large envelope waiting in the mail pile from Robyn. I opened the envelope and there is a hand-written note attached to a special marathon edition of the Gold Coast Bulletin, the local newspaper. In the note Robyn said, "I saved this paper for you, no doubt your name is in here along with many of your friends, I guess. Hope your trip to the US Convention was fruitful, Kind regards, Robyn."

Now that is follow up! How did she make me feel sending that special edition of the paper? Over the moon! The first thing I did was search for my name, then my wife's name and then the names of my friends that had all taken part in events across the race weekend. What a lovely, thoughtful gesture and yet what a simple thing to do.

Following up is an essential thing you must do, not only that, you must put your personal stamp on the follow up, just like Robyn did.

There are some follow up techniques to avoid of course. I spoke for a Chamber of Commerce on the south side of Brisbane. I noticed a woman going studiously around the room, introducing herself to every single person in the and exchanging business cards. The interaction was brief, "Hi, I'm Denise, from Denise's Book Keeping (OK, that's not her real name), do you have a card?" At this moment she produced her card, gave me a brochure and then took my card. Then she moved on to the next person in the group.

When Denise swept on to the next victim, I thought, what a peculiar way to conduct business, no attempt at a conversation, no interest in what I did, nothing, just give me your card. The next day, it became even more bizarre, I received an email from Denise that went something like this.

"Hello, it was so nice to meet you at the Chamber of Commerce yesterday morning. As you may recall I am an independent book keeper and specialize in small business book keeping and monthly BAS reporting." She went on to describe more about her services. The email finished with, "Because you are a valued associate, I am willing to offer you a discount of 20% off your first month's book keeping. In order to qualify for this amazing offer, you must book your first appointment within 7 days." She then finished, "Looking forward to working closely with you, best regards, Denise."

This approach is just so wrong at so many levels. She starts, "It was so nice to meet you, "Yeah right! All she wanted was my contact details, she made no effort to "meet me" at all. She then called me a "Valued Associate" really, it sure didn't feel like it when she flipped out her business card waiting for me to give her mine. I could go on for ages dissecting this horrible effort at relationship building and selling. Learn a good lesson here, do not follow up in the style that Denise has developed, unless of course you wish to turn people away in droves.

Think carefully about your follow up strategy, choose what works best for you, whether that be by email, in writing, or by some other method. Make your follow up style unique and efficient, something that is easy to do no matter where you are in the world.

Relationship Building Action Steps

1. Remember to follow up and do what you said you promised. Send that article, your book, or whatever.

2. Do not follow up with advertisements, monthly specials or general marketing offers unless you promised to do so. No one likes Spam, it will hurt your relationship more than enhance it.

Chapter 14

Trust Me, He'll Be Back

When it came time to fit the roof on the house, we had the supply part covered, as I wrote about earlier, Moose, one of the kindy dads delivered roofing iron for a living and he organised the raw materials for me. At a very good price too I might add, thanks Moose!

When it came to fitting the roof; I was stumped. I didn't know any roof plumbers and I wasn't game enough to do it all on my own. Of course, I simply went with the relationship I already knew and trusted; Moose. I asked Moose if he knew anyone that could fit the roof for me. Straight away Moose had the perfect recommendation for me. His mate Mick was a roof plumber and he had an offsider Pete.

It turned out that Pete was a fireman and a roof plumber. He was bored with full time plumbing so got a job as a fireman and then worked both jobs simultaneously. Most firemen work four days on and three days off. When they are on, they live at the fire station and are literally on call twenty-four hours a day. It can be a high-pressure job fighting fires, so the firemen are given three days off after each shift to rest. However, what used to happen back then though was that most of the guys had some sort of second occupation, that they moonlighted in for some extra money.

The roofing iron was delivered on a Monday and on the Tuesday Mick and Pete showed up to start fitting the roof. They were likeable blokes and had many funny stories to tell of sliding down freshly laid roofs after a shower of rain. To make corrugated iron, flat iron is put through an industrial strength roller machine that bends the corrugations into the iron. To facilitate this happening, the iron sheets are coated with a fine rolling oil, which is still present long after the iron is fitted to the roof of the house. The combination of a little bit of rain and the rolling oil can make for some interesting adventures if you are a roofing plumber apparently.

I clearly recall Pete regaling me with the story of the day he and Mick had been working on a freshly laid roof after a shower of rain. Pete was working above Mick when he lost his footing and slipped down the roof. Calling out he slid hurtling toward Mick. Mick looked up just in time to be collected by Pete as he skidded down the slippery iron and they both fell off the roof to the ground and landed in a puddle fresh from the rain!

They looked at each other and groaned, checking to see that all their limbs were present. Then they heard an ominous noise. A split second later, their power drill was following their path, clattering down the roof slowly, inexorably, making its way toward them and their puddle. Once they heard the splash beside them, Pete said you've never seen two blokes scatter faster in your life. You see, a power tool, two soaked plumbers and electricity doesn't make for a healthy combination. Lucky for them the circuit breaker tripped the power off at the same time the drill splashed into their puddle.

Like most of the tradies on site, I laboured for these guys; initially helping them lift the sheets onto the roof while they screwed the sheets down, fixing each sheet with just the bare minimum of screws to hold it in place. The full screw down would happen once all sheets were in place. The job was progressing well.

The roof was progressing well that is, until Pete had to go back to work. He'd done his three days and by then I sort of knew enough that I could labour for Mick until Pete returned four days later. Well, that was the plan.

On the Friday Mick didn't show up as expected. I called his mobile and left a few messages and no response. The weekend came and went and on Monday still no Mick. I rang Moose and explained the situation, fearing I would have to hire another roof plumber. Maybe I had said something to offend the guys? When I explained the predicament to Moose, he simply said, "Trust me, he'll be back."

I think it was the Tuesday, maybe even the Wednesday of the following week when early in the morning, a car I didn't recognise pulled up in the driveway. A rubbery man, half fell, half poured itself out of the car. It was Mick. He had obviously seen better days and it was only when I got close that I understood what was wrong with him.

Mick had been on a bender. Unknown to me, however well known to Moose, Mick loved a drink. Rum was his favourite tipple and apparently, Mick had done his best effort over the past three or maybe four days to get well and truly plastered. When he spoke, he slurred his words and I was lucky there were no naked flames nearby as I swear he may have caught fire!

"Lindsay, solly (sorry) mate," slurred Mick. "I'll be back on the job tomorrow".

I have to say I was nervous, I called Moose straight away. His reassurance was clear and simple "Don't worry mate, I trust him, he'll be back". Sure enough at 7a.m. the next day, in drove Pete, with Mick in the seat beside him. They both got out greeted me and went to work. The roof was finished in record time after that. Sober, that guy was a great roof plumber, as for the rest, I still don't want to know!

Other people may have sacked Mick on the spot, I trusted Moose and he trusted Mick, so you can see how this trust thing works. It's a huge key to making relationships work, both personal and business.

Give Trust to Get Trust

One of the most important processes that works alongside 'Finding the Common Ground' is building trust. Building trust is a critical part of relationships and without trust you will not progress to the next level in a relationship. The next obvious question is "Well, how do I build trust?" Trust can be built over time or it can be given as a gift almost.

Trust as a Gift

Let's start with the latter, giving trust. This was one of the critical elements I employed when I built the house. I didn't know that many tradesmen, though I did know a couple that I trusted deeply. When I asked them for a recommendation, I trusted the person they recommended to me. Consequently, trust can be given, if I trust you and you recommend someone to me, the trust I have in you passes to them.

This theory works well, though of course there may be shortcomings. What happens if the person recommended to me is a dud, doesn't deliver or delivers poor service? Well, an obvious outcome is that I may no longer trust the person making the recommendations to me. This could impact on our relationship either short term or long term.

If you plan to give the "gift" of trust, make sure that the person you are recommending is also trustworthy and will do what they say they can do. If they don't, your relationship with the other person will certainly be compromised.

Earning Trust

As I said earlier, trust can also be earned and in fact this is the usual method most people employ. Earning trust can take several forms:

- Simply Turning Up
- Build Micro Moments of Trust
- Keeping Promises
- Becoming an Authority

Let's examine these individually.

Simply Turning Up

Trust is usually slowly earned and it's up to us to prove we are trustworthy. One of the simplest ways to do this is to turn up! Interestingly we tend to trust people who are a large part of our lives. When I was a child my mother trusted me to go anywhere in our street and play as she trusted the neighbours. One of the prime reasons for this level of trust was that they were around and part of our daily life. We knew them and they knew us. The more we saw of them, the more we trusted them. In fact, my parents were the first residents of our street and as each new house was built my parents introduced themselves to the newest neighbours and made them welcome. They literally knew everyone!

As time wore on, some of these neighbours became a part of our lives in some way, others not so much. We knew their kids, what jobs they had, we saw them almost every day. We trusted them.

Step out of my neighbourhood now and go to the world of business.

If you want to build trust with other business people and hopefully sell them your goods or services, you must turn up. For example, if you belong to a Chamber of Commerce or a Professional Association, you can't attend just one meeting and hope to do business with one or more of the members. You must regularly attend the meetings, get them used to the idea of who you are and what you do. The more they see you at the meetings, the more comfort they have in you and the more they will trust you.

This is also part of most advertiser's strategy when they advertise on TV or in the print media and now social media. Coca Cola always has a huge advertising campaign to keep their brand in the forefront of our mind, so when we are thirsty and we approach the drinks fridge at the shop, we go for the brand that we are familiar with and trust.

Keeping Promises

Trust is also the outcome of kept promises. If you say you are going to do something and you do, you build a small amount of trust with that person. If you meet someone at your Chamber of Commerce and have a nice conversation and at the end of the conversation you promise to do something for them, you'd better deliver!

It could go like this, you are talking about an article you read on Facebook just this morning, the other person says, "I would love to see that". You say, "Sure, I'll email you a copy when I get back to my office".

This is your chance to build some of that trust, make sure the minute you return to your desk, you email them the article in question. If you don't they may not remember, or worse still, they will remember and know that when you promise to do things, you may not really do as you promise.

Build Micro Moments of Trust

If trust is the outcome of kept promises, the next logical step is to create moments that allow you to keep your promises or give you an opportunity to prove your trustworthiness. I call these Micro Moments of Trust.

A Micro Moment of Trust is an opportunity for you to deliver on a micro promise. One of the simplest forms can be getting someone a cup of coffee at a business function. If you think about it, it is fulfilling a promise and builds you credibility and trust. There are literally hundreds of ways to deliver Micro Moments of Trust.

If you aren't sure, here's ten ideas to get your creative thinking started:

- Offer to get someone a drink at a business function.
- Recommend a great restaurant.
- Open a car door for someone.
- Offer to let someone slip into the line-up for the food buffet ahead of you.
- Hand the next person in line from you at the buffet a plate for their food.
- Send someone an email with an interesting article you referred to during an earlier conversation (without promising to do so earlier).
- Introducing a visitor to another guest that could potentially do business with them.
- Send someone a thank-you note, in your own handwriting.
- Call someone up and offer them a lift to attend a business function together.
- Recommend a great website or blog.

Becoming an Authority

Many modern entrepreneurs have built enormous levels of trust with their clients and yet they have never met. They have become a trusted authority by providing information and advice freely. Becoming an authority again does not happen overnight, however by giving a cumulative supply of useful tips, tools and ideas, your target market will begin to know you, then like you and finally trust you.

The next outcome here is they will trust you enough to purchase your products.

Note the steps here to becoming an authority; know, like, trust. You can't jump over any of these steps in the journey to building trust.

Build Trust by the Changing Environment.

Another way to build trust is to do so by changing the environment. If you are trying to build trust with someone and perhaps it's not quite working the way you would have hoped, try changing the environment. Create a new relationship environment, change the situation.

I have a client who services the credit union industry, they do all of the back-end processing of the financial transactions for a large number of credit unions. They don't work for all credit unions...yet! However, they are trying hard to build trust and develop relationships with the credit unions that they aren't working with yet.

One of the Directors of the business, Harry, said to me "Lindsay, we haven't had any luck getting to these guys through the normal business channels, so we are going the alternate pathway." This alternate pathway was to interact with their prospects in different environments. At the annual Credit Union Conference, these guys always had a trade stand. It was always the biggest and they always served food.

Harry loved his food and he figured that food was also a way to build trust and do business. They were famous for serving hot dogs and other snacks at their booth. People queued up for ages to get a free hot dog and Harry told me they had many Micro Moments of Trust happening whilst serving hot dogs. Of course, he also followed up with marketing material after those encounters, again building his trust profile with the prospect.

There are many different ways you could attack this one, just look for an opportunity to do something different with your prospect. Why not invite them to one of these events:

- Football
- Tennis
- Dinner
- A theatre show
- Your industry conference

Of course, the list goes on and it's only as short or long as your imagination.

In December each year an architectural firm I work with takes their staff on a magical mystery tour. The owner is one of the best bosses I've ever met, he genuinely cares about his staff and works very hard to build trust. He knows that if he has a good relationship with his staff and he looks after them, they in turn will look after him.

Back to the magical mystery tour. Each year in December all staff are informed that they will be having their Christmas gathering over a certain Friday, Saturday, Sunday. They are told to be at work Friday with a packed overnight bag and expect to be home again on Sunday afternoon. That's all they are told, though sometimes hints or clues are given to build the surprise.

Finally, the day arrives and at the last moment as they head to the airport or board the bus or whatever, they are told where they are going for the weekend. Whilst they are away, all food, drinks and accommodation is taken care of. Can you imagine how much trust and loyalty is built over this weekend?

Think about how you could change the situation to create a different opportunity to build trust with a prospect, client or your staff.

Relationship Building Action Steps

1. You have to give trust to get trust.

2. You can be given trust as a gift, however make sure you honour that gift and do a great job.

3. Trust is the outcome of kept promises, remember to always do what you said you would do.

4. Think about how you can build trust in small steps with new clients.

Chapter 15

The Key 4

I mentioned in the first Chapter about DNA and the structure of DNA containing four basic building blocks which create our genetic makeup. This determines our physical, physiological and emotional behavioural traits.

Let's step out of the world of chemistry now and into your business and think about the DNA of your relationship management system. I believe that you need to surround yourself with four key business allies. These business allies will form the building blocks of your relationship management system and will be the key to sourcing business outside of your normal sphere of influence. These will be like-minded people, who all share the same target market, yet must not compete in any way with each other. I call these people the Key 4.

The Key 4 like the four building blocks of our DNA make up the building blocks on your relationship-based business and if you train them correctly, will bring you an endless source of referrals and positive relationships to your business. The Key 4 Group are your ultimate wingmen!

Why have I chosen four people, it's simple, any more is too many, social scientists tell us that we all know at least 250 people. If we boil that down further, we are probably in regular contact with about 10% of that group, that's twenty-five people. Of the twenty-five people, we have regular contact with, not all would be suitable to work closely with. Yes, we bump into them regularly, however we may not have the kind of synergy needed to be part of a Key 4 Group.

I believe four is the best number as it is easy to keep closer contact with a smaller group and build the trust necessary for the group to function properly.

Choosing Your Key 4

Let me give you an example of a Key 4 Group. A Real Estate Agent I was coaching wanted more business and was lamenting about the lack of a good referral culture in their region. I encouraged her to form a Key 4 group. The first question I asked her was, "Who is your target market?" Her target market were couples wanting to buy residential property in the Ferny Hills, Ferny Grove, Keperra, Bunya, Grovely and Mitchelton area. They must be willing to spend between $400,000 -$1,000,000 to secure their property.

Next, I asked; "Who else shares that target market and is not in competition with you?" We brainstormed a list and came up with, mortgage brokers/bankers, insurance brokers, building and pest inspection services, commercial photographers, furniture removalists, landscapers, pool builders, pool inspections services and conveyancers or solicitors.

From this list, we pared it down to the essential services that would be most beneficial and decided ideally her Key 4 would consist of a mortgage broker, a solicitor, a building and pest inspector and an insurance broker. Next, we went through her database and identified suitable candidates for each of the identified skill sets. This whole process took about 45 minutes and very quickly we had the bones of a Key 4 Group ready.

Clearly this is not an onerous process and one that you can do for yourself right now. Once you have the categories sorted, you need to think about the individuals that will fill each slot. Choose carefully.

Start with individuals that you already have a working knowledge of and that you have comfort dealing with. Ask yourself these questions about them:

- Do you share the same target market as them?
- Do you share the same business and personal values as them?
- Do they understand the law of reciprocity?
- Do they need more business and are they open to doing business by referral?
- Are they open to new ideas and concepts, a different way of doing business?
- Are they open to training and being coached?

Once you have your list of names and you believe they meet the criteria, you can begin the process of recruiting them to your team. Keep an open mind as to who may belong to the group. Perhaps one of your Key 4 could know or have a better candidate for the group than the person you have identified. Be open to alternate suggestions and remember the goal is to form the best Key 4 group, not just for you personally, the members must all benefit, otherwise the group won't function at its best.

Training Your Key 4 Group

The goal of the Key 4 Group is to look out for each other, build relationships and refer business to one another. For this to happen effectively you need to know as much as possible about their business so that you can give them the best targeted referrals. Make it easy for your group members to train each other about their businesses.

You can use these five simple questions as the basis of the training process:

- How would I identify the perfect prospect for you?
- How would I describe your unique selling proposition to my customers?
- What are your best products and services that you want me to promote?
- What trigger words or phrases should I listen for from my clients, that will tell me they are an ideal referral for you?
- Once I identify a prospect for you, what is your marketing process to move toward a sale?

I also encourage members of the Key 4 Groups to visit each other's business premises, so that they can tell their customers or likely prospects all there is to know about their Key 4 member. Invest the time necessary to learn all you can about these four people, remember the initial training period may not yield a whole lot in terms of referral business, however it will deepen the relationships and trust among the group.

Operating Your Key 4 Group

Your Key 4 Group, should become the central element of your marketing and customer service efforts. It's entirely up to you how you run this, it could be very formal and structured or perhaps more informal. The overall intention though must be to add value to the group members and your respective customer bases.

One of the essentials of the group is the introduction process. In the example above about the real estate agent, it was so easy. Every new couple that wanted to inspect property were asked some simple questions. Have you thought about how you will finance this purchase to get the best deal for you? This question was often met with this typical response "Well we've been banking with Westpac (or whoever) for years, so I guess we'll just go ask them for a loan.

This is when the real estate agent would jump in with "Probably the worst deal you can do is with your current bank, I have a mortgage broker I work closely with. He has access to a large range of financiers and often beats the banks interest rate by a country mile, would you like me to introduce you to him?" At the prospect of saving money, the response is usually 99% positive. Then the real estate agent chimes in with, "In fact, I have a small group of dedicated suppliers that specialize in everything that you will need to purchase this house and move in, how about I introduce you to my whole team. I'm sure we can save you a lot of time, stress and money."

Can you see how simple, yet powerful this strategy could be in your business too?

I recommend that once you have done the initial training, you schedule regular meetings with this group to keep in touch and to keep the motivation running high. Set aside at least two hours and maybe more at a regular agreed time each month to meet and review the group. Some groups that I coach have the following agenda:

- Each member has 3 minutes to recap on business generated and referrals given over the last month within the group. Time spent -10 minutes.
- Each group member spends 15 minutes talking about their business, what's trending, where they need help or referrals. Time spent - 75 minutes.
- One member runs a 20-minute educational session on some aspect of their business product or service. The goal here is to keep the group up to date with what you do. Time spent – 20 Minutes
- Group agrees on the next steps and sets a date for the next meeting. Time spent - 10 minutes

Total time spent 120 minutes, or two hours. It's entirely up to the group however, you could easily spend more time together. You will find as the relationships deepen, business challenges and problems are often brought to the table and shared and solved by the group. If this happens, it is simply an added bonus for the members of the group.

The Referral Process

Some groups struggle at first trying to figure out how to get the referral process working. The whole idea is that you all share the same target market and do not compete, this then means you can easily share clients also, as there is no way one member could steal them away from another member.

A simple process is to identify a small group of clients and target them for a specific member each month. Choose say, ten clients and contact them with the intention of introducing them to another member of your Key 4 group. This could be done in the form of a mail out campaign, an email campaign or better still a personal conversation with each person.

Let's go back to the real estate agent and her Key 4 Group. The real estate agent could make a list of ten existing clients that have purchased houses from her over the last twelve months. She is working with the insurance broker to help them get more new clients. The personal conversation would go like this:

"Hello Jacqui, it's Denise French from French's Real estate here, how are you? I'm ringing because it's been 10 months since you moved into that lovely new house and I'm thinking there will be a few services that you will be reviewing shortly, one of which will no doubt be your house insurance."

"I've been working closely with Merv Brown from Brown's Insurance Brokerage and he has managed to save a number of my client's money by reviewing their insurance policies before they fall due. It's a simple process for Merv to do a quick quote for you for your house and contents. Is that something that might interest you?"

"It is! Great, I'll get Merv to contact you straight away to organize a quick phone consult."

You get the idea and I'm sure you can think of the appropriate words to say for your business and train your Key 4 member about what to say on your behalf.

The Key 4 in Action

Of course, you should never miss an opportunity to promote someone that is part of your Key 4. One of my own Key 4, Pamela Wigglesworth from Singapore, has walked alongside me on the journey of writing this book and has produced her own manuscript called "The 50-60 Something Start-Up Entrepreneur" How to quickly start and run a successful small business.

Pam recognises that across the globe, there is an increasing forced exodus of 50 to 60-year-old employees happening within organizations across multiple industries. In her book she offers a concrete, step-by-step process that will show you exactly how to start and run your own small business. Clearly the ability to build relationships quickly is a part of that, however Pam drills much deeper and provides practical tips, tools and ideas on how to survive and thrive.

It's the natural next step if you are at all entrepreneurial, after you have finished reading this book. You can buy copies here: https://books2read.com/u/mYgjxW

Relationship Building Action Steps

1. Identify who will be your Key 4 Wingmen.

2. Write a shortlist of candidates and choose just four people that share your target market, yet do not compete with you.

3. Take the time to train your Key 4 and learn about their business too.

4. Set regular Key 4 meetings to keep each other up to date, on track and focused on building and growing your businesses.

Chapter 16

Ten Proven Relationship Tactics

Now that you have the Ten Step model in place, you know how to get into a relationship quickly, work with a Wing Buddy and have your Key 4 in place, I want to take you on to the advanced level of working a room. Getting started is often the hardest part, once you are comfortable about getting into conversation and keeping the conversation moving along there are a bunch of other tactics that you can use to engage with and enhance your relationships in the room.

Pace & Lead

Years ago, I did a Neuro Linguistic Programming (NLP) training program and we learned the concept of Pacing and Leading. For those of you not sure what NLP is, I'll explain briefly. It's a sophisticated communication skills program based on the three most influential human components: neurology, language and programming. One of the first skills I learned was that to communicate better with someone you have to enter their map of the world, or putting it simply, be more like them. The 'more like them' was primarily aimed at your verbal language and your body language.

Pacing and leading can be done either physically and/or verbally. To make it easy to understand, let me tell you about Phil.

Phil, a manager that I once worked with, identified his boss's speech tempo as being much faster than his. This typically made Phil uncomfortable and nervous and this resulted in his thoughts becoming scattered. Phil decided to try pacing and leading his boss's tempo. Although it was not comfortable for Phil to speak fast he managed to pace his boss's tempo. After about five minutes Phil slowed down his tempo. His then noticed that his boss had also slowed down and Phil continued to slow down until he felt comfortable talking to his boss.

Phil concluded that his boss was truly a flexible person. Perhaps even more so than Phil. In addition to pacing and leading tempo you can pace and lead volume, tone, gestures, posture, breathing, representational systems and eye-accessing cues. Basically, you identify a pattern in the other person, match that pattern and then subtly change the pattern. Observe with your eyes and ears what happens next, if the person does not follow you then resume the pace and try again momentarily.

So now you know what to Pace and Lead means, you can now apply it at a business function. When you are talking to people, you must pace and sometimes you have to lead. If you enter a group, take a moment to listen to the pace of speech, note the energy in the group, listen to what they are talking about, listen carefully for the words being used. When appropriate, you can join in the conversation, at the exact pace the group is taking. If you come in too fast or too slowly, you will certainly not fit in as easily.

If you sense that you are pacing the group well, then and only then, you can take the lead and move the group energy to a different level. I've seen experienced relationship management experts join a group and lift the energy dramatically within moments of entering the conversation.

Catalyst for Conversation

I'm a great believer in having a catalyst for conversation that I wear or take with me to business functions. I am a member of Professional Speakers Australia, the premier body for professional speakers in Australia. I'm a Hall of Fame speaker and Life Member of this group and very proud of my association. When I'm wearing a suit or jacket, I always wear a lapel pin which is a microphone and symbolizes my membership of this group.

Here's the interesting piece, you would be amazed at the number of people that talk to me and gaze at my lapel pin. Sooner or later, they say, "Is that a microphone? What is that for?" This gives me a few opportunities and depending on who I'm talking to and where I am, will dictate the response I'll give. Let's assume I'm at a networking event where I'm looking for opportunities to seek work. I will say, "Oh that is my Professional Speaker's Australia pin, I speak at conferences and seminars for a living and this pin signifies that I am among some of Australia's leading professional speakers."

Typically, they will ask, "What do you speak about?" This then allows me to tailor a message aimed at the target market I'm shooting for at this particular event. I may then go on and talk about the national and international speaking industry and maybe about being a Hall of Fame speaker and a Life Member. Of course, if I'm at an event with my wingman, they will tell the group all about my prowess in the industry, it's always so much more powerful coming from another person rather than you directly.

One of my colleagues has amazing printed documentation about the services he offers. He always carries a full colour A4 sized printed booklet about these services and never misses and opportunity to show a prospect what he can do for them. This may sound overzealous; however, I've seen him produce this document and then I see his prospects' eyes go saucer- shaped as they gaze at the high-quality document, jam packed with great information about the services this guy offers, plus amazing testimonials from his satisfied clients.

He uses this same document to introduce himself to prospects by email. So, for example if you meet him at a function, he will say something like, "Oh, if you like I could send you some information about what I do." This is always met with "Oh sure, that would be nice". Once he sends the material through, he sure has their attention and it almost guarantees another meeting to discuss how they can work together.

A catalyst for conversation works at so many levels.

They Look Interesting?

Have you been at a business function and seen someone that just looks interesting and you don't know who they are? Maybe they are surrounded by a bunch of cool people, maybe it's something about the way they dress, you just want to know who they are. Here's where experienced relationship builders hit the road running. Go straight to the event organiser or someone who knows everyone and ask, "Who is that person?" Once you get a name, then find out some more about them, ask the organiser about them, go check out their LinkedIn profile or perhaps their Facebook page. Figure out if they are worth meeting, could they be a prospect for you or your Key 4? Then go and introduce yourself.

Here's the thing though, you must use some of your newly gained knowledge to grab their attention. It could be as simple as, "I saw on your LinkedIn profile that you are a member of Rotary, I used to be a Rotary President many years ago. Rotary has opened lots of business doors for me. Can you tell me about your experience in Rotary?"

Tom, the event organiser tells me you are a marathon runner, I ran my first marathon on the Gold Coast recently , one of the hardest physical things I've ever done. What's the best marathon time you've ever run?

Of course, the aim of an opener like this is to get them talking about themselves as much as possible, remember the 80/20 rule. Get them talking about themselves and they will love you for it.

Listen for the Conversation Clues

I have a friend, Abby that works in a small office with just five other people. Twice a year her boss Danielle takes all the team away on a weekend retreat to review what they have achieved and to plan what they will do for the next twelve months. The retreat is as much a reward for effort as it is a planning event. Danielle treats her staff generously during the weekend, taking them out for dinner each night and she also provides a nice lunch with lovely snacks to feast on during the planning sessions. They go to an island resort and in Abby's words there is nowhere else to go, so no-one escapes! It's not that Abby doesn't like the retreat, it's just that her boss Danielle takes her husband Ethan along for the weekend also.

I was talking with her recently and she was bemoaning the fact that another of these weekends was approaching. Being curious, I couldn't help but ask what the downside of this event was for Abby. "It's Danielle's husband," she said. "He's such a stick in the mud, it's so hard to get him engaged in a conversation and last year I got stuck sitting beside him, it was a major bummer" she said. "What do you talk about over dinner?" I asked. "Oh, mostly work stuff, we often continue our planning discussions, though in a more informal sense."

"Have you considered for a moment that Ethan may not be interested in the business or perhaps may not know enough to contribute?" I asked. Abby pondered this for a moment. "I hadn't really thought about that, I just assumed that as he was Danielle's husband, he would know all about the business. I prompted, "Here's an idea for you, why don't you try to figure out what he's interested in and then ask him about that?" "It's worth a try" Abby mused.

Two weeks later I caught up with Abby for coffee and she was bubbling over with enthusiasm. "Tell me, how was the planning retreat?" I asked. "It was the best weekend ever" she said. "I did exactly as you suggested, I figured out what Danielle's husband Ethan was interested in and bam! I couldn't shut him up, he talked and talked. He was such fun too." "OK, fill me in" I said, "How did you figure out what he was interested in?" "I had to do what you told me, listen more, talk less." Abby went on with her story.

"We walked by a shop front on the beach on the afternoon of the first day and we noticed a sign advertising fishing charters." Ethan stopped and said out loud to no-one in particular, "Will you look at that beauty," marvelling at a photo of a huge coral trout being held up high by a guest on one of the charters. "Instantly I thought this was my opportunity, "Do you like fishing?" I asked.

That was it, the flood gates just opened. He loves fishing, it turns out he has a small tinny and loves to fish on the weekends, occasionally he goes on a deep-sea charter like the one we were looking at. For the rest of the weekend, all I had to do was ask a fishing related question and Ethan's eyes lit up and he was off. The most interesting part was that he had so many funny fishing stories, he became quite the life of the party holding court, telling us about one funny fishing misadventure after another."

Once Ethan revealed his passion for fishing, two of the other staff revealed they liked fishing too and suddenly there was a common topic for all of us to talk about, apart from the planning stuff.

What's the lesson to be learnt here? Like Abby, you must keep your eyes and ears open for clues on what the key to someone else's passion is. They will often blurt it out subconsciously, a bit like Ethan did, or you will hear it in their voice. When they talk about a topic for which they have some passion, you will hear their voice change. They may use a higher pitch and they may talk faster. You simply must be observant. Remember a good relationship builder always listens more, talks less.

Harness the Jargon

Have you ever been involved in a conversation with two or more people from the same profession and suddenly you notice they are almost speaking a foreign language? They are using words or jargon that is just foreign to you. My son-in-law, Sam and my brother-in-law Terry are both IT dudes. They love getting together at family functions and talking business, the problem with that is, most other people trying to follow this conversation are going to fall asleep pretty soon! I'm exaggerating of course, however this can become a real issue if you are at a business function and you find yourself in between two boffins discussing their latest research into whether a tape worm knows which part of the gut it is currently inhabiting and why. It's not hard to tell what their passion is, the tricky bit is joining into the conversation in a meaningful way.

The key here is to know just enough to get by, without sounding like an impostor and or an idiot. I have a long-time friend, Debbie Wiggan. She has a full-time job assessing and rating jobs for employers, yet her real passion is art. She started painting years ago and really enjoyed the process. She joined an art class and today is still friends with some of the women she started with in that art class. The more interesting part for me has been seeing her progress over the years with her art, she's amazing.

Recently she held an exhibition with three of these friends she started with all those years ago. The exhibition was held in an old church converted into a gallery at Paddington, an inner-city suburb in Brisbane. In preparation for the event I brushed up on my artist jargon , so that I would sound at least interested and perhaps even a little bit knowledgeable. I didn't want to stand out to be the rank art philistine I probably am!

I asked Debbie for some clues, "What do artists talk about?" I asked. "They talk about the medium they work in," explained Debbie. "That could either be oils, water colour, acrylics, charcoal or pen. There will also be some photographs on display, so photography is now considered art in some circles. That photography could also be film or digital, so be careful about that," she advised.

I asked her about a term I had heard; 'mixed media'. She explained that none of her friends would be displaying any mixed media work, which was a combination of traditional art, oil, watercolour etc. with the addition of other materials, like collage, pen or chalk.

I felt that after my briefing with Debbie that I was qualified to "do" art speak and at least engage in a conversation using the correct terms or "jargon".

In every industry, hobby or profession there will be local jargon that may be hard to understand or pick up initially. In one of my first jobs I worked in a customs agency. My role entailed going to the Customs House every day and paying the duty to clear the goods from the wharf on behalf of the importer. It was a complex process with lots of paperwork and often the paperwork was in triplicate. One of those forms in triplicate was submitted to the Customer, the first sheet was in full colour, the second was plain white and the third was yellow. The Customs department kept the original and then we kept the white sheet, which wait for it was called the "Blue" and the yellow sheet went to the transport company for collection of the goods.

Let's back up a moment, yes, the white sheet was called the "Blue," go figure, tricks for young players. It took me a while to get that when my supervisor was asking for the "Blue" he really wanted the white sheet of paper. Local jargon. Turns out that once upon a time the "Blue" was really that colour and somewhere along the line it had changed colour, however the jargon hadn't kept up with the change. An extreme example, however, it demonstrates the point that every industry or occupation has strange terms that often, only insiders know about.

Of course, language changes worldwide and even when we visit countries where English is in widespread use, there may be times when tuning in to the accent makes a difference even though you are speaking English. I was working in Singapore and for those of you that haven't had the chance to visit, most of the population speak English very well and in fact they have a local version of what the locals call Singlish, Singapore English. It's called Singlish also because it's spoken in a kind of sing/song way. A lot of words have "ah" or "lah" added on to the end of them, for no reason. A simple OK, becomes "OK'lah".

I called a taxi to the complex I was staying in and the taxi driver was a lovely friendly man and as we drove out of the complex we had to go through a boom gate. To get the gate to lift the driver had to press a green button. We arrived at the gate and the driver seemed confused so I said, "Press the button." He pressed everything but the green button. Next moment I hear myself saying, "Green'ah, Green'ah". Sure enough, the driver understood perfectly what I was saying and pressed the correct button and the boom gate lifted.

Sometimes we must learn the local words relevant to the industry we are hanging out with and yet other days we need to learn how to say those words in order to make ourselves understood.

Read the Paper

(You used this anecdote in Chapter 9)My Dad was a safety equipment salesman before he retired. I remember when I was still living at home Dad would religiously read the sports pages of the newspaper every morning before he left home to go to work. Dad was a big

Rugby League fan and followed the local football competition closely over many years. However, one day, I noticed he was avidly reading the soccer results and a long article on the woes of the local soccer team in the national competition.

When I noticed this I asked, "Why are you reading about the soccer team?" "Oh, I'm going to visit Sam Simpson today" he said. "Sam is a big soccer fan and if I'm going to have any credibility talking with him, I have to know about the soccer". At the time this seemed strange to me, however it now makes perfect sense. If you want to get into relationship with someone, find your common ground. Dad didn't have much common ground with Sam, though he soon found out Sam was passionate about his soccer, so Dad became equally as passionate, when he visited Sam. Well, at least he put on a reasonable effort and could keep up a conversation with the guy, when he talked about his favourite team.

The lesson to learn here, is to read the paper, if nothing else scan the headlines so that you know what's topical, so you can hold a conversation when you are at your next function. What's that I hear, you don't buy the paper, that's OK, just go to your mobile phone and Google news headlines and any number of news services will pop up with the latest headlines, so you can appear somewhat knowledgeable when a topic comes up in conversation.

A dear family friend and mentor of mine, Keith Nielsen was a canvas product salesman during the seventies and eighties before he retired. I remember him telling me about many of his clients or prospects and one in particular was memorable. Keith told me that he called on this guy once a month and the meeting would always last an hour. Keith would be ushered into his client's office and knew never to mention his products or ask for a sale, he simply asked how this guy's Australian Rules football team was travelling. He would then sit back and listen to this guy whinge about how bad his team was, how they couldn't take a mark, how they couldn't kick, how they couldn't catch a ball, how they hadn't won a flag in twenty years, you get the idea!

Keith could almost time his watch by the sour epistle and at about the 55-minute mark, the client would glance at his watch and say, "Oh well, we can't talk football all day, better see what we need this month." He would then proceed to rattle off an order of supplies he wanted to buy from Keith that month. Keith taught me, sometimes you just must sit still and listen to have a great sales relationship!

Tune in to Their Troubles

Do you belong to a professional association? Do they send you a magazine or newsletter by email regularly? How often do you take the time to read it rather than just scanning it? It's amazing what you can find out about your industry just from reading the regular publications your association makes. Take this one step further and think about building relationships. Now, what could you learn from your industry journal that may help you in a conversation with a colleague or prospect at some stage in the future?

I'm a member of three professional associations. One is my industry body, the other two are target markets for me and I do a lot of work in these two industries. One of these is the Venue Management industry. I'm a member of the Venue Management Association and by their affiliation with their USA cousins, I am affiliated with the IAVM, the International Association of Venue Managers. I get two paper magazines sent to me each month with articles of interest from the industry; current events and trends, all documented and readily available for me to read. Next, each association has an email newsletter and other publications online, which again give me more information and data about my target market.

In Australia, they advertise job vacancies every week, so I can keep an eye on vacancies. Great information when you are talking with a client and you know that they are recruiting at the moment. They know you have real interest in their business when you keep up with that level of detail. The USA association publishes a great online newsletter with a Q&A section. Here any member can post a question about literally anything and get answers from their peers all around the world. This is a perfect vehicle for me to offer advice and cement myself as an expert in the industry.

What industry publications are you reading every week?

What about the good old newspaper? Do you get the paper delivered every day? I bet you read the headlines first then have a system where you work your way through your favourite pieces of the paper. My sports mad mate, Rob Wiggan always turns to the sports section first of course, me, I tend to read from the front page until I hit the sport, then I stop reading!

Here's my personal challenge to you, try something different tomorrow, read another section of the paper first and you may just find out something interesting that you can talk about at your next business function. In fact, you may find that instead of being left out of the conversation, you become the centre of attention as you are suddenly eminently qualified to speak up about the topic, because you read about it in the paper that very morning.

I know some people that just don't even buy the paper anymore. My eldest brother Neville reads his online now, my mate Jacob, doesn't buy the paper in print or online, he says it's just full of negative stories and advertising that he doesn't need to read. He has the same view when it comes to television news, so he's a drop out and when he's at a business function he proudly proclaims he doesn't care! Personally, I admire his resolve, however, saying I don't care, does simply alienate you from a large section of your potential client pool. The reality is most people do care and do have an opinion.

I ran my first ever marathon in July 2017 on the Gold Coast, it was a tough race and I'm proud to say I finished. I didn't finish in the time I had planned; however, it wasn't from lack of preparation, more physical stamina on the day. You see I had prepared, I began training on the eighth of January 2017. I ran 110 times and totaled 692.2kms in my preparation. As part of my preparation and training I spoke to other runners, I researched training for a marathon online, I subscribed to running newsletters, I bought running books and I haunted the News Agent every month waiting for my copy of Runners World magazine. I became thoroughly immersed in the world of running.

The thing I noticed at the news agent whilst scanning the shelves for my Runners World magazine was the amazing variety of hobby or special interest magazines available, cycling, weight lifting, swimming and surfing. Next there were a plethora of gardening magazines, cooking magazines, knitting and crochet and the list goes on and on.

Do you have a client or a prospect that has a special interest, perhaps it may be worth investing a token amount of money at the newsagent to find out more about their passion, so that you can converse with them a little easier at the next business function you attend?

Nothing Beats a Shared Experience

Have you noticed that like attracts like? I was at a wedding earlier this year and noticed a group of men at a table in the back corner, all hunched in closely around a tall bar table. Curiosity got the better of me and I sauntered down to the back of the room to find out what the attraction was. It was a transistor radio and they were all listening to a football game, apparently, some poor thinking relative had scheduled a wedding on the same day as a big rugby union test match between Australia and New Zealand. For those of you who don't follow the rugby, um, that would be me, this game was a big deal. The Wallabies and the All Blacks are arch enemies and the rhetoric that goes around these games is legendary.

These men were engaging in what we all love to do: sharing an experience, especially one which is enjoyable or a common interest.

In conversation, everyone loves it when they can chime in "Me too." When my son Drew was a teenager he played junior golf in a competition at Wantima Golf Club, he loved his golf. My job was to get him there every Saturday morning ready to tee off by 6.30am. That meant rising at 5.30am, levering a sleepy teenager out of bed, force feeding him some breakfast, then driving him to the course. Once he and I were both awake, we really did enjoy the experience. I usually volunteered to walk around with the kids, as they needed a parent to keep them on track, to keep them moving forward and not getting distracted.

I was at a barbecue one Saturday evening, yawning quietly into my beer, when the guy beside me asked if he was keeping me awake! We laughed and I explained in excruciating detail why I was feeling a little weary as I had been up so early to take Drew to golf, walked the course with him, then chipped a few balls around the backyard that afternoon in practice with him as well. I lamented the chore of being a golf Dad.

I should have known when I saw the knowing look on his face, I should have realised when he so readily agreed when I said what a chore it was waking so early on a Saturday morning. It all became clear when he said those simple words "Me too." He too had a teenage son and he too had been up early and he too had spent the morning walking up and down the side line at a football field that morning. He too had spent time in the backyard practicing moves with his son that afternoon.

Do you think we clicked! We sure did, we had so much in common. Interestingly he had refrained from jumping in at the start of my story. He had graciously allowed me to go all the way through my sorry tale while he patiently listened. Finally, he had revealed his similar yet not the same experience. What a gentleman!

I pondered on this conversation later and decided it was a very useful technique to develop and use while at business functions. Too often I've seen people jump in and cut through someone's story with their own version. Just take some time, let the other person have their say, waiting is such a compliment. I was keen to give this a try elsewhere.

Not long after, I bumped into a business friend Emily, at a Chamber of Commerce Meeting and she was looking great, sporting a tan and just looked relaxed. I complimented her on the tan and she said, "Oh, I've just had two weeks' holiday at the beach." "Where did you go?" I asked.

She launched into a long description, she had stayed at Bulcock Beach in Caloundra just one hour north of Brisbane. She loved Bulcock Beach as it's not a surf beach, it's opposite the northern tip of Bribie Island and the best part about the beach was that on the incoming or outgoing tide you could do what she called, 'Floating'. You simply dived into the water and floated on top of the water. The tide would take you along the beach until it was time to get out of the water and walk back along the beach to where you started and you jumped back in again. Such lazy bliss on a holiday!

She went on, right across the road from Bulcock Beach was a strip of restaurants and the building she stayed in. You could decide if you wanted to eat in your unit or walk downstairs and choose from about a dozen different food styles and prices, right at your doorstep. She told me she started each day with a vigorous walk north around the headland to Kings Beach and from there you could walk all the way to Moffat's Beach, which was nine kilometers further north.

She mentioned on the Sunday; they close the main street at Caloundra and hold a market and there's an eclectic range of stalls offering all sorts of exotic food and goodies to buy. When she finally ran out of steam, she said, "Have you ever been to Caloundra?" I smiled, "Yes, we holiday at Bulcock Beach for a week every January around Australia Day.

"What!" she squealed "Why didn't you say something?"

Truthfully, I replied "I love that region and it was lovely to hear what you like about the area, it's interesting that we have so much in common." I didn't mention that I had been testing out my new theory and I proved that it's true, nothing beats a shared experience.

Next time you are in conversation and you have shared the same experience, let the person recounting the story enjoy their moment, knowing how much joy it will bring to the conversation when you reveal that you two have shared this experience. They say patience is a virtue and in relationship land, patience is also a relationship builder.

Laser Like Focus

The key to a good, long term relationship with people is to come across as credible, knowledgeable, competent and confident. Remember, first impressions count and the more you establish yourself that way, the longer the first impression will last. There are times when you enter a new group and you literally must start again to create the right impression.

How do you come across as knowledgeable, credible and confident in that first impression moment? The answer is in what you do with your eyes. Go get your favourite DVD movie, fast forward to the part where there is a heavy piece of drama. Watch carefully and you will see the actors do a curious thing with their eyes, they don't blink. Clever presenters on current affairs programs do this as well, they carefully stare at the camera while they recite their most important story without blinking. Go check it out, it's not easy, however you can train yourself to do this too.

If you can talk without blinking it's almost hypnotic, you can almost put people into trance. It's because all your ideas seem to be presented as one connected unit and they literally can't think of how to break them apart. They should take in your whole message, instant credibility.

Get yourself in front of a mirror and go practice this, it does work and it can be learned.

I first heard of this concept from Michael Grinder, a presentation skills coach based in the USA, he said, the average person blinks somewhere between six and eight times per minute. He further explained that research showed that you blink to moisten your eyes and you also blink to figure out "What and I going to talk about next". Actors can deliver their dramatic lines without blinking because they have memorised their lines and they don't have to stop and think about what comes next, they are simply speaking by rote.

As human beings, we have been taught how to blink, whereas our favourite actor has a script, which they have memorised. They almost have to be trained to blink, whereas we have to be trained not to blink.

Cultivating this Laser Like Focus will give you credibility when you meet people for the first time and of course it will be useful for reinforcing your prowess in an established group. When you speak, you will command the attention of the group.

Gestures Don't Lie

In my previous career as a human resources consultant, I interviewed a lot of candidates for roles both in the public and private sector. Over time I became quite proficient at guessing when people were telling the truth or not. I was caught out in my younger days. I remember clearly interviewing this guy, he did so well at the interview, answered all the hypothetical questions and seemed so confident and comfortable. We recommended him for the role, only to find out he was a great salesman, when it came to promoting himself, sadly though he was a poor performer. He was lazy, had a poor attention to detail and was basically a pain in the butt for the section to which he was recruited. I learnt a good lesson from that experience .

Over subsequent years I perfected my interviewing skills and learned to watch for signs that the applicant may be bending the truth. I interviewed one applicant and when we asked him to give us an example of how he had done an activity in the past, he adopted some curious behaviours. He was sitting cross legged, suddenly he shifted legs, then he took a sudden interest in his finger nails, he lowered his gaze, avoiding meeting our eyes while he spoke and picked at the quick on his fingernail. When he finished his "story" he looked up again.

Curious about this sudden change in behaviour, I went back to talking about stuff I knew that was true. I talked about some trivial details where he was currently working, the floor he worked on and how many staff were employed in his section. Of course, he was very comfortable talking about this information and he gazed sincerely into the panels' eyes.

Going full circle, I took him back to his example of previous work experience and asked him to clarify something I had just thought of. Sure enough, his posture changed, his eyes went down and he started to fidget with his finger nails again.

I couldn't say for sure, however I had a fairly good hunch that the example he was quoting was a fabrication or a large embellishment. I made sure that we did very thorough reference checking on this guy and you guessed it, his story did not hold up. His referee could confirm that he was indeed embellishing his ability and achievements in this area.

So how does this relate to relationships? Make sure that when you are engaging in serious conversation with someone at a business function that you refrain from excessive or sudden changes in behaviour or outright fidgeting. What may seem to you like an innocent itch or niggle may seem like you are skirting the truth to your conversation companion.

Relationship Building Action Steps

1. Practice these relationship tactics and use the top 3-5 that resonate best with you.

Chapter 17

Relationships in the Cloud

Building relationships isn't restricted to face-to-face or the meeting room, in fact these days it's possible to build huge relationship-based networks from the luxury of your home office, through the magic of the internet. There are literally hundreds if not thousands of social networking sites online and each site will have its own community, culture, focus and etiquette.

I used to believe that Facebook was for fun and LinkedIn was for Business. However, this no longer applies and each site has advantages and disadvantages depending on the target market you are shooting for.

I've built quite an online following and have thousands of connections; however, the value is not in having the connections, it's what you do with those connections and how you do it that is more important. Remember that relationships are about interaction and connection, so you must find a way to stay connected and in a relationship with the connections that you have.

In the early days of Facebook and Twitter, I recall online suppliers selling Facebook "Likes" and Twitter "Followers". The problem with these was they were pretty much useless in terms of real relationship building. The "Likes" amounted to an ego trip and the "Followers" didn't care two hoots about what you posted, so it really was an ego trip for the purchaser and a profit centre for the promoter.

You must build your following by entering a relationship based on the Relationships Guy 10 Step Model. Start with finding the Common Ground and then quickly move to providing the P.S. That is, some Positive Service. Build relationship by becoming a trusted source of good information and support for your followers. Give them a reason to come back again and again to visit your site in order to interact with you.

Let's look at the three main social media sites I engage with online, Facebook, LinkedIn and Twitter.

Facebook

Facebook was launched in February 2004 and was initially limited to the students of Harvard University. It became open to the public in 2006, when anyone over the age of thirteen was allowed to become registered as a user. Once registered, a user can add friends, post status updates, photos and videos. They can also exchange messages and receive notifications when friends make posts or update their profiles.

Users can also join common interest groups based on their hobby, work interest, or other interests to share information, or simply keep up to date with current issues and trends. Users also have the ability to categorize their friends into groups such as "close friends" or "hobby group friends" or whatever, depending on their affiliation.

Facebook has become the most popular social networking site in the world with over two billion users worldwide as of June 2017. As well as personal pages, Facebook rolled out business pages in May 2009, enabling business owners to take part in this social networking phenomenon. Most business owners would now have a personal page and a business page of some sort on Facebook.

Setting Up Your Profile

As I mentioned earlier, I used to regard Facebook for fun and not business and my profile reflected that position until about five years ago, when it became obvious that Facebook was a serious business medium and you can easily be judged and misunderstood if your profile and postings are not appropriate for the business image you wish to project.

Having said this, the first thing you need is a decent photo or avatar that represents you. Note I use the word avatar; you don't have to use a photo, in fact go and check out my personal Facebook page or my business Facebook page and you will see I use an avatar or caricature of myself. When I started out in business in 2000 I had a great creative team and they came up with a caricature of me standing and presenting, this has evolved over time.

About twelve years ago I moved away from the caricature and a lot of people commented, "What happened to the little man?" It seems I had created something uniquely me, so at the next rebranding I went back to a caricature or avatar. This has served me well and sets me apart in terms of my brand. What works for me, however may not work for you. Whatever you chose to make sure that the photo or avatar is of professional quality and represents you well.

Having said all that, the banner in the background being my avatar is a photo of me presenting in real life on a stage in Kuala Lumpur, Malaysia. Choose a photo and banner background image that best suits your brand.

In your profile setup, you can choose different levels of sharing and determine who sees what you post, just remember that if a friend can see your post, they can share it with about a million or more other people, so assume that whatever you post is going to be seen by the world at large.

The next most important part of your profile is the About section. This is like your biography or bio on LinkedIn and details your employment situation, your education history, your location and contact information. Make sure that you have your website and your mobile number listed here, just in case someone may wish to contact you.

What are you sharing?

What you share may depend on whether you are sharing on a personal or business page. Let's start with your personal page. Obviously, you are going to share what's happening in your world currently, that could include photos, memes or video. It's OK to include some business posts on your personal page as well, in fact most people are happy to see what you are up to in the business world as well as your personal world.

The same rule applies for a business page, it's OK to post some personal stuff, it shows that you are human. I go back to the Pareto Principle rule or the 80/20 rule. Stick to 80% personal if it's your personal page and 20% business and vice versa for your business page.

A business colleague of mine posted regularly on her business page and then became very ill, she was absent for a week or two and only had a few minor scheduled posts during that period. When she recovered, she went to her business page and posted saying she had been unwell and apologized for the gap in her information flow. What happened next amazed her, she was overwhelmed with words of kindness, likes and comments about her illness and recovery. It seemed her followers wanted to know about her personally as well as business. From that day forward, she always made sure to apply the 80/20 rule and includes some personal posts.

Another business colleague of mine is a mature woman with grown up children and a string of grandchildren. In every stream of her social media she always makes some mention of her family at some stage throughout each month. People see her as being "real" and "normal" and absolutely relate to her human approach to running a business and being part of a large family.

Friend Requests

When you set up your profile initially you would no doubt have invited a group of people you know to become friends. Once you get rolling, Facebook regularly suggests people that you may want to be friends with based on who you are friends with now. If you belong to a professional association like I do, there are often many, many people you could connect with that are part of your association. Each time you become friends with someone new, Facebook will suggest some of their friends for you to connect with.

You can go "friend hunting" and trawl through your friend's pages, looking to see who they are friends with and send them connection requests. You can wait for your list to grow organically of course and again it depends on what your purpose is for joining Facebook.

I personally reject few requests as I believe you can never have too many people in your network, however I am aware of other people who are very fussy about whom they accept as friends on Facebook. Again, it depends on why you have joined Facebook to begin with. For me it's about business and personal, so I don't mind having heaps of friends. Many friends give you access to even bigger networks when you are looking to promote an event or something similar.

Facebook Tips

Being in relationships is all about interacting, so make sure you stay connected to your friends and followers. Post interesting and perhaps sometimes thought-provoking posts, rather than selling stuff all the time. Remember the 80/20 rule.

Allocate an amount of time every day where you will concentrate solely on Facebook. I usually check in at the beginning of the day and then another two or three times depending on my day. Typically, I will check in over lunch while I'm eating to see what's happening and then again after dinner while I'm relaxing in front of the TV. I could check in more depending on what I'm up to, so if I'm between meetings and have ten minutes to kill, I'll check in. When I say check in, I simply mean, I'll go scroll through a bunch of posts, perhaps check if I have any comments or likes on one of my posts or check other posts I'm following.

If you have posted an item and people are commenting, make sure you support the relationship and perhaps comment back to them, or at the very least 'Like' their comment. Avoid being a Facebook stalker i.e. reading a bunch of posts and not liking or commenting. Remember relationships are a two-way street, you get back what you give out. If a friend posts something, like it or comment and comment positively. If you have something negative to say I believe it's best to do that privately, offline or not at all.

Remember Facebook is always open and the world continues to turn, so posts will continue to be made right across all time zones. When I get up in the morning I get a lot of posts from my USA friends as their day is already half over, as the day progresses, so do the posts from various countries in various time zones. Another reason to check in throughout the day.

Posting interesting questions issues or problems can be a good way to get attention and attract followers. If people see you as fun and controversial, they will want to follow you. Of course, you don't have to be controversial, you can simply be topical, either way make sure you post interesting stuff to gather a following.

Posting photos and video is now a sure-fire way to get 'Likes', comments and generate interest. A long wordy post is more likely to be ignored in favour of an interesting photo or video. One of my most watched posts is when I filmed a chef in an Italian restaurant make a pasta dish inside a huge cheese wheel at our table. He poured in liquor and set it on fire to melt the cheese, then added the pasta and other ingredients, swirled it around then served it up. Amazing to watch and it captured the imagination of my followers, so many comments and likes.

Use Facebook to promote your other social media pages by posting when you have just Tweeted, or published a Blog article or a LinkedIn article. Add a link to your post so your followers can go read your article and perhaps register to follow you on your other social media sites as well.

Remember Facebook changes its operating policies and rules regularly, keep up with the changes so that you don't breach any of their rules.

LinkedIn

LinkedIn was launched on the 5th May 2003 and today is recognised as the place to go for business people to connect and to do business together. Not only that, it is used extensively as a site for recruiters to source candidates and potential candidates to display their talents to recruiters. There are over 500 million members across 200 countries in LinkedIn, with around 110 million active account users. A great place to establish key relationships for you in your business.

LinkedIn encourages business owners to create company pages and individuals to create profiles showcasing their talent and achievements. Individual members use LinkedIn to share their professional profile, almost like an online resume, network with other business people, promote their business prowess, join groups of like-minded professionals and to grow their network.

LinkedIn can be used to source new business, find a job or connect with peers and share ideas. Given the versatility of LinkedIn, it is a perfect place to engage in relationships building with your target market. To do that however you must have a profile.

Setting Up Your Profile

Start off by following the simple process to get started. Add your employment history, your bio, your education. If you have been recognised by your company, industry, or community with any special awards, list them here too. Remember whatever you write must be appropriate to the target audience you are hoping to connect with. Keep your "special" sense of humour under control here, this is a business site and readers expect to read a business style profile.

This profile may be the catalyst for you to snag that new job, or perhaps tip you over the edge to win that amazing contract with the prospect you have been courting for some months now.

Make sure you have a good headshot photo to display, it's better to have these done professionally rather than try to find a photo you have already and try to make it work. I've seen Profile pictures with a mysterious hand draped over someone's shoulder, which obviously was a good friend or colleague cropped out of the photo. Make sure the photo is a current one of you as well. I have met many men and women that look a LOT older in real life than the glamour shot photo they have posted on the online profile.

Once you post the photo, look at your profile online and ask yourself, "Would you do business with that person?" If the answer is "I'm not sure," change the photo.

When you read some profiles, it's easy to see the person has had bucket loads of experience and has a long list of previous employment or exciting projects they have been involved in. What if you are just starting out and don't have such a list? That's OK, start off with your educational details, list your school and university details. List any part time employment you may have had and highlight the transferable skills you have because of that employment.

Once you have done all this, go back over what you have written and make sure it's all spelt correctly and the grammar makes sense.

Free Versus Paid

The beauty of LinkedIn is that you can use it for free or pay extra and take advantage of extra services. I was a free user for many years while I built my network and it's only in the last year that I've paid for the Professional Version. I consider the AUD$500 for the yearly subscription a great investment and it has enabled me to connect with so many more people and do some serious business.

One of the advantages of the paid version is that you can search for and find people in specific industries, locations or companies. You can message a lot more people each day and you can see exactly who has been viewing your profile, both key parts of good relationship building activity. It all depends on where you are in your business as to which format you choose. If you are expanding your network and trying to connect with people, the free version is enough. If you want to get serious and want to connect deeper, find more people and make sales, then the paid version is the way to go.

Just Start Connecting

I believe the best way to connect is manually, that is send every individual a personalised invitation to connect. There is a generic connection request, though my belief is that relationship builders always send a personalised message. LinkedIn suggests names of people you should connect with. You can always go see who your friends are connected to and invite their connections to join your network.

When I joined LinkedIn, I wasn't sure what I was supposed to do, so I made as many connections as I could. In fact, in the beginning it was a game, a business colleague of mine, John Bellamy and I had a running competition to see who had the most connections on LinkedIn. I would sit at the kitchen table at night while my wife was watching TV; connecting with people.

I just looked for people who were second connections and sent them a simple message. "It seems like we have a lot of connections in common, thought we should connect directly". This had about a 99% success rate, sometimes I never heard back from people, though mostly they just connected. If you are using the paid version, you can search for people in an industry and then connect with them.

For example, I do a lot of work in the Venue Management industry, which means I'm looking for connections with people that work in sporting and entertainment venues across Australia and the USA. I can search a company name, or a venue name and see who comes up.

The largest venue management company in Australia is AEG Ogden and they are one of my long-term clients. I could search AEG Ogden and then connect with anyone that works for them. One of the newest venues they manage is the International Convention Centre (ICC) in Sydney. They have recruited from far and wide to staff the new venue. I could search for the ICC and see who I haven't yet connected with and send them a request.

Once you begin to build your network it is surprising what happens next, people start sending you connection requests and your network grows organically. I never say no to a connection request as my belief is that you can never have too many people in your network.

I was talking with someone recently and they told me they only connected with people they knew. In my mind this defeats the purpose of LinkedIn. It's designed as a business network tool and the idea is to connect with people to expand and grow your network and hopefully build trust and do business with a percentage of that network.

Occasionally you get a bogus connection, I connected with a female "Business Banker" according to her profile recently and once we were first level connections, she messaged me suggesting that I was a very handsome man and that she was looking for "company". Clearly this person needs a new pair of glasses and is probably a Nigerian scammer looking to scam money out of me. My next step was simply to disconnect and block them.

I have also had several people connect and then message saying they have an amazing business opportunity for me. These people are usually network marketers and my strategy here is to politely decline their generous offer.

There is a network marketing group active on the south side of Brisbane that connect via LinkedIn and then invite you to a networking function at a hotel. The invitation says you will get to meet a lot of like-minded people and make even more great connections. I politely decline these invitations and if necessary disconnect and block the connection.

Once you have established a network, take every opportunity you can to promote yourself and your membership of LinkedIn. You could do this by including the LinkedIn Logo at the bottom of your emails in the signature block and alongside the Facebook and Twitter Logos. Of course, those same logos should appear on your blog page, your website, your Facebook and Twitter pages.

Endorsements

LinkedIn offers a unique way to highlight your strengths to visitors inside your profile under the heading Featured Skills and Endorsements. You can list your key Skills and have others endorse you for that skill. I've limited my skills to just nine core skills, LinkedIn keeps suggesting other skills I could add and even suggests to other people to endorse me for skills I have not yet added. My belief here is that less is more.

I stick closely to my main message and only have the essential skills listed. I've been to some profiles where they have twenty or more skills listed. What's the message here? Are you a specialist in one field of a generalist in many? I prefer to be a specialist.

A quick way to get endorsements is to give endorsements. I still regularly search my connections, read their profile and endorse them for say three skills they have listed on their profile. I chose three because I want to be genuine and endorse them for something that I have experienced of them and so that it is a real endorsement. Spend just ten minutes a day endorsing other people and you may be amazed at what comes back to you. Remember you get back, what you give out.

Recommendations

If you want to stand out on LinkedIn and in the business community, get some good recommendations on your profile. I started out tentatively with this one, again I wasn't sure of what to do. I started with a few of my trusted clients and asked if they would be willing to endorse me. To save them time and knowing that the answer was probably going to be yes, I even wrote a simple recommendation for them, based on a piece of work we had done together.

My message went something like this "I know you are busy and to save you some time I've drafted a recommendation for you, based on the XYZ Project I delivered for you recently. If you are comfortable with what I've written, all you have to do is post it on my profile. Of course, if you want to amend it in any way, I will be delighted to receive your recommendation."

In my experience nine out of ten people simply posted what I wrote, the tenth person often went and added even more positive superlatives to what I had written, the ultimate compliment.

Like endorsements, another good way to get recommendations is to give recommendations. This strategy takes a little longer and can be executed in one of two ways. The first way is to simply write a testimonial about one of your connections saying something complimentary about their work. It's not hard to come up with a compliment and it doesn't have to be a huge essay, just two or three sentences. I always put my name, my position and my company name at the bottom of the recommendation too. My theory here is this way we both get some promotion.

The second way is to contact someone you have worked for and ask for a recommendation and say that if they do a recommendation for you, you will do one for them. The perfect act of reciprocation. If they post a recommendation for me, I usually wait about 24 hours before I return the favour so the recommendations look "organic" rather than manufactured.

Share Riveting Content

Sharing content is a great way to attract more connections and to stay in touch with the connection you already have on LinkedIn. Again, there's more than one way to do this, you can repurpose other people's content and post it on your feed with a wise comment.

As an example; one Friday, I posted a blog on my website. This blog was almost immediately picked up by a follower of mine and reposted on their LinkedIn feed. Within 24 hours it got over 1,000 views on their LinkedIn feed and then I noticed one of their followers had reposted the blog onto their feed.

If you share the right content, your name will be spread far and wide and then people come back to you and connect so they can read your articles directly.

Of course, I could have and indeed since have posted that article directly to my feed on LinkedIn. Posting articles, blogs, memes, anything of interest to your target market on LinkedIn is a great way of maintaining your relationship with your network.

Join Groups and Contribute

Another great way to build connections is by joining a group in LinkedIn. They literally have over one million of them to choose from, yes, that's a lot of choice. There are so many to choose from, so be careful that you don't spread yourself too thinly. Join a group that is relevant to your business and then get involved. Read the posts made by others and make informed comments about what they have written.

The more you get involved the more likely it is that people will follow you, connect with you and when you post, comment on what you have written. Be careful when you post in a group that your message is useful to the group and not just thinly veiled self-promotion, no one likes a braggart, so keep the content high and the promotion low. By simply posting good thought provoking work, you will be promoting your brand.

Participating in the right groups can easily cement your reputation as an expert in your chosen field. Use your participation wisely, offer value, build your network.

Your LinkedIn Daily Ritual

I have a daily ritual to manage my LinkedIn network, which I would like to share with you.

Here's the ritual:

- Login to LinkedIn.
- Create a post and upload it.
- Check your messages and respond accordingly.
- Check who has viewed your profile and send them a message if appropriate. If
- someone views your profile, they may want to hire you.
- Check Connection Requests and send them a personalised message welcoming
- them to your network.
- Respond to any comments on your posts or articles.
- Check at least three other updates and make an informed comment.
- Check the groups you belong to and make comments.
- Send a message to targeted connections with a call to action to attend your
- webinar, read your lead magnet or book an appointment.
- Send ten targeted connection requests with a personalised message.

If you do this every day, I guarantee you will build a bigger, stronger network and get business from your efforts.

Twitter

Twitter was launched in July 2006 as an online social networking service. Registered users post short messages limited to just 140 characters known as 'Tweets'. Only registered users can tweet;

however, anyone can read the tweets. Users access the service through the Twitter website or via their mobile device app.

Twitter rapidly gained popularity worldwide and by July 2017 was hovering around 328 million active users every month. These users tweeted around 6,000 tweets per minute and around 500 million per day. That's a lot of tweets!

Interestingly the pivot point for Twitter was at the famous South by Southwest Interactive Conference in 2007. This conference is a technology focused gathering held each year in Austin Texas. Conference organisers placed big screen TV's in the hallways of the conference venue and enabled users to tweet and have their tweets read by others on the big screens. People began following the action and tweeted more, to be part of the drama playing out on the TV screens. Speakers at the conference mentioned what was happening and event attendees jumped on board causing the number of tweets to rocket from 20,00 to 60,000 per day.

Getting Started

Setting up an account is easy and takes very little time. Once you join you will be asked to follow a small number of accounts to get you started. Twitter will help you out here and even suggest some users for you. You can also search for topics that interest you and follow accounts that you find there.

Next Twitter will search your email contacts to find contacts that are already on Twitter and will suggest you follow them. This is usually a good place to start

Twitter for Business

Twitter is a great place to promote your business and to make connections and deepen relationships. It is considered normal twitter etiquette that if someone follows you, you follow them back. I personally always check out the person's profile before I follow them back. There are spambots out there (robots that send out spam or bogus messages) that are designed to gather followers by this automatic follow back etiquette, so be careful.

I only follow people that I consider interesting or someone that is my target market or is aligned with my business field or purpose. That really does leave the field wide open for connections.

Twitter is like a good business function, you get to 'meet' interesting people, have interesting conversations and sometimes have your thinking challenged by contrary opinions. If Twitter is like a business networking function, then similar rules apply. Keep self-promotion to a minimum, you remember that person at the breakfast that never shuts up, or worse that tries to sell you something at your first encounter. Don't be that person on Twitter!

Better to make some connections, get to know each other a little first, listen more, talk less, find some common ground and then implement the good old P.S. (Positive Service) Strategy.

Listen More, Talk Less

Initially Twitter should be about listening more and talking less. People often ask questions and this is a great opportunity to be able to share good information. Share helpful tips, interesting stories or anecdotes that add to the conversation started by that person. This is a great way to expand your network. You can then move on to add some conversation starters of your own. Ask for some information, share a link to an interesting story, ask for comments, opinions and feedback.

At this early stage, it sometimes feels like you are at a business function with very few people present, almost like you are talking to an empty room, though as you find a following, you may be surprised at the responses you get after you make a tweet.

Find the Common Ground

The best way to get into relationship quickly as you know by now is to start with what you have in common with other people and talk about that. I believe it works the same on all social media sites, including Twitter. The easy way to find people with similar interests is to search using a hash tag (#) or the @ symbol. You can search topics, people, places, pretty much anything using these symbols on twitter.

So, go search on your passion, interest or industry and see what and who you come up with. Start following a few people and see what the conversations are like.

The P.S.

One of the critical parts of any new connection is the P.S. The act of a positive service. On Twitter, this could be sending someone a direct message, saying thank you, or sending them a link to further information, or whatever you might normally do when you deliver a P.S. at a business function.

As part of the P.S. make sure you follow up. Think about who you want to cultivate in your network and follow up and stay in touch with them on twitter. Keep an eye out for their tweets, comment or respond as appropriate, keep the conversation going. Share the tweets of the people you most enjoy and remember, what you give out, you get back.

What to Tweet?

Starting on Twitter can be a little scary, so think about breaking down the style of tweets you might make into categories, then brainstorm what you might say under each of those categories. I work with the following four categories when I am planning my tweets:

Informative

As the name implies, you are going to share some facts, news, business tips or information which will be useful information for your audience.

Supportive

This is your opportunity to support other people and their causes. You could promote other people by mentioning them and their work or you could promote events, issues or causes that interest you.

Inspirational

Inspirational quotes are all over the internet and Twitter is not immune. Try using a different approach and write your own inspirational saying. Choose one or more of your favourite motivators and share them with your audience.

Entertaining

Everyone loves a bit of fun or a laugh, so take a moment to share something entertaining for your followers. Why not find a humorous meme and share it, or a link to a cartoon or video?

Retweets

If you read a tweet from someone and you like it, you can retweet it. This forwards their message on your feed and is a nice way of promoting other people and their work. This is especially good for deepening relationships. If I see that someone has retweeted my work, I check out their profile, thank them and if I'm not already, begin following them.

When you retweet, you are unable to comment on the tweet. If you want to comment on the tweet you can recompose the tweet starting with the letters RT. This enables the original user to see that you have commented and retweeted their material.

Direct Messages

You can send direct messages to people on Twitter. Often after someone starts following me, I will send a direct message thanking them for the follow and wishing them well. Direct messages can also be used to share a quick private message with someone else.

Automating Twitter

There are several online tools which make posting on Twitter easier and allow you to setup tweets in advance and then send them at a predetermined time and date. Two of my favourites are Hootsuite and Buffer. Hootsuite can be used to schedule tweets and also post status updates on Facebook and LinkedIn.

Buffer has the same abilities and can also help you to schedule the tweets. Buffer figures out the best times of the day for you to post your tweets and status updates.

Some would argue that scheduling tweets is not what Twitter is all about, however the reality is that busy people still want a voice and a presence. The secret is to make sure that you tweet occasionally in between your scheduled tweets to change the pace and keep your followers interested.

Relationship Building Action Steps

1. Set up your chosen Social media platform, either Facebook, LinkedIn or Twitter.

2. Build your network by invitation or organically by providing value.

3. Decide your strategy for LinkedIn, will you use the free version or pay for the extra privileges.

4. Endorse and recommend other people and they in turn will mostly return the compliment with an endorsement or recommendation.

5. Share great value adding content at all times.

Conclusion

By now you will have realised that this relationship thing is really not that complicated. It is however essential if you plan to interact with other people. Whether you are a leader in a large organisation, a sales person that wants to make budget or a business owner that wants to be successful, being able to get into relationship with other people inside and outside your business is essential for your ongoing success.

I started this book with the premise that our ability communicate has been disrupted by the digital revolution and I whole heartedly believe that if we aren't careful our ability to communicate face to face will be severely impaired and impacted by hand held devices.

I've given you some simple steps to take to enhance your ability to engage with others and communicate face to face and also via Social Media. Take the opportunity to sit for a moment and think about how you can implement the tools and techniques in this book to enhance your business and even personal relationships.

Next, take action! I've included Relationship Building Action Steps at the end of each Chapter, now go back over those steps and make sure you are doing everything in your power to engage, expand and energize your business relationships.

I'm in the process of writing more books about business networking and referrals, all based on the common ground of relationships. So why not go try some of these ideas out and let me know how it goes for you. I would love to hear from you and perhaps include your story in one of my future blogs or books. You can drop me a line at lindsay@lindsayadams.com

I sincerely hope that this book has helped you in some way and I look forward to hearing from you. Stay tuned for my DNA of Business Relationships online course. You can find out more about that on my website www.lindsayadams.com

Good luck and go out there and build some amazing relationships!

Acknowledgements

This book has been "in process" for about two years now. I would like to acknowledge the team behind me that has made this project become real at last.

First, I must thank my wife Debby for her unending love and support, she believes in me and has been there for me throughout this process, thanks Debby, you are the bestest!

Next ,I would like to acknowledge my book buddy, Pamela Wigglesworth, in Singapore. We have walked along the book writing pathway together and spent many hours brainstorming, debating and supporting each other, thanks Pam. You can purchase Pam's new book, "The 50-60 Something Start-Up Entrepreneur" How to quickly start and run a successful small business, by going to this link https://books2read.com/u/mYgjxW It's a great read.

I would like to acknowledge Dixie Maria Carlton, good friend and creator of Authority Authors. She has been persistently nagging me, digging me in the ribs and cheering for me throughout this adventure, thanks Dixie.

I also want to thank my good friend and business colleague from Toronto, Canada, Christel Wintels, she is the one that pushed me over the finish line with some full and frank feedback one morning whilst we were on one of our regular Skype calls, thanks Christel.

Finally, I would like to thank my many friends both locally and internationally from the professional speaking industry. You have been fountains of knowledge and inspiration and I am proud to say, I am now an equal among you as a published author.

Follow "The Relationships Guy", Lindsay Adams

I invite you to stay in touch with me through my various Social Media Channels. I love to hear from and interact with my clients, friends and followers, so stay engaged with me via the following platforms.

Amazon

Connect with me on Amazon and find out when the next book, The DNA of Business networking will be launched. I would love your thoughts and ideas as I develop the next book and of course a nice review of this book on Amazon would be gratefully appreciated.

Facebook

My Personal Page "Lindsay Adams" can be found at the following link. https://www.facebookkcom/lindsay.adams.505

You can also join me on my Business Page "Lindsay Adams Speaker" for all the latest news ideas and tips about relationships building, business networking and doing business by referral.

LinkedIn

Connect with me on LinkedIn and read my current articles on business relationships, plus interact with my 11,000 plus connections. https://www.linkedin.com/in/lindsayadams/

Twitter

Follow me on Twitter to get some quick, sharp observations about business relationships. Connect with me

@Teamocracy

YouTube

Subscribe and follow me on my YouTube channel, see video of me presenting at conferences and sharing my ideas and concepts. www.youtube.com/LindsayAdams

About the Author

Lindsay Adams CSP, Global Speaking Fellow is a practiced speaking professional, workshop facilitator and business relationships specialist. With over 20 years word of human resources and business relationship experience, Lindsay's focus is on building effective relationships and generating more sales in less time by doing business by relationship.

How does he do this?

Lindsay Adams is able to identify what stimulates staff. In his presentations he coaches his audience to help them achieve peak performance. Lindsay offers solutions to help increase sales and maximise an organisation's "Relationship Building Power".

Lindsay's customised keynote presentations and workshops are tailored to meet specific organisational needs and provide educational information in an entertaining way. He provides the tools to assist you to retain, re-train and relate to staff, and focus on teamwork and achievement.

Lindsay's Experience

Lindsay has worked with executive teams, individuals, entrepreneurs and business owners across Australia, Asia, Europe and the United States. He won't just 'tell' you the principles of the topic, he will help you put them into action. His content rich presentations and follow-up advice help you and your team apply life and business changing principles to their everyday behaviour to achieve long term success and goal fulfillment.

Accreditations

Lindsay is a Master Practitioner in Neuro Linguistic Programming and holds many management and training accreditations. He utilises these in his presentations and consulting work with a diverse range of clients.

Lindsay was the 2009-2010 International President of the Global Speakers Federation and a Past National President of the Professional Speakers Australia (PSA). In March 2013 he was awarded a life membership of the PSA in recognition of his speaking prowess and service to the industry locally and internationally. He holds the first ever Global Speaking Fellow designation award.

The Global Speaking Fellow is the highest membership category of the Global Speakers Federation and the only internationally recognised designation for professional speakers. This designation guarantees that you receive a professional presentation every time.

Organisations like Sumitomo, Reuters, Suncorp Bank, Singapore Press Holdings, Brisbane City Council, Bendigo Bank, Linfox, Brisbane Entertainment Centre, Queenslanders Credit Union, Rio Tinto, Ungerboeck International, Uniting Care Health and many more have hired Lindsay to assist them with building and enhancing business relationships with their teams, their stakeholders and their clients.

Today

Lindsay is happily married to Debby and has two adult children that grew up and left home...Woohoo! They are both in happy relationships and each has produced a beautiful grandchild that Lindsay and his wife can dote over.

Lindsay writes his blog and is featured in numerous magazines and media. To find out more about Lindsay, his programs and workshops, go to www.lindsayadams.com

Email Lindsay at lindsay@lindsayadams.com

What is the DNA of Relationships?

Most people attend business functions because they know they must, yet they don't know how to start a conversation and quickly get into relationship with others. Like all skills, it's something that can be learned. In **The DNA of Relationships**, you'll learn how to become better at meeting strangers, starting a conversation and quickly moving into an engaging and profitable business relationship.

Lindsay Adams, 'The Relationships Guy', walks you through techniques like:

- How to ask just one question and relax while others do all the talking
- Finding the common ground in a topic that contributes to an engaging conversation
- How a P.S. (a small act of positive service), will have people beating a path to your door to do business with you
- How to give and get trust to increase your credibility and your sales
- How to identify and recruit your **Key-4™**: the ultimate wingman strategy for even more referrals

You'll discover an easy to implement structure to overcome those all-important, yet often terribly awkward, first moments at a business function, enabling you to confidently meet prospects, make connections and clinch sales.

Lindsay Adams is 'The Relationships Guy' and has been building and refining his business relationships for more than 30 years. His relationships have helped him to build a house, travel the world easily, have a happy marriage and enjoy diverse and exciting lifelong friendships.